KNOW WHAT
YOU WANT—
and Get It!

KNOW WHAT YOU WANT—

and Get It!

NORMAN MONATH

CORNERSTONE LIBRARY
Published by Simon & Schuster, Inc.
New York

Published by CORNERSTONE LIBRARY
A Division of Simon & Schuster, Inc.
Simon & Schuster Building
Rockefeller Center
1230 Avenue of the Americas
New York, New York   10020

CORNERSTONE LIBRARY and colophon are registered trademarks of
Simon & Schuster, Inc.

10   9   8   7   6   5   4   3   2   1

Manufactured in the United States of America

Library of Congress Cataloging in Publication Data

Monath, Norman.
  Know what you want—and get it!

  1. Success. I. Title.
BF637.S8M59   1984   158'.1   83-26204
ISBN: 0-346-12627-4

The author is grateful for permission to reprint selections from the following publications:

How to Make it in a Man's World. Copyright © 1970 by Letty Cottin Pogrebin, published by Doubleday & Co., Inc.

The Art of Selfishness by David Seabury. Published in 1979 by Cornerstone Library.

The Meaning of Your Dreams. Copyright © 1969 by Valerie Moolman, published by Cornerstone Library.

Wake Up and Live! Copyright © 1936 by Dorothea Brande, published by Simon & Schuster, Inc.

Lateral Thinking. Copyright © 1970 by Edward De Bono, Harper & Row, Publishers, Inc.

The Art of Creative Thinking. Copyright © 1982 by Gerard I. Nierenberg, published by Cornerstone Library.

Inside, Looking Out. Copyright © 1971 by Harding Lemay, Harper Magazines Press.

Playwright at Work. Copyright © 1953 by John van Druten, published by Harper & Brothers.

The Enjoyment of Laughter. Copyright © 1936 by Max Eastman, published by Simon & Schuster, Inc.

"Self-Sabotage in Careers, a Common Trap," by Bryce Nelson, *The New York Times*, February 15, 1983. Copyright © 1983 by The New York Times Company. Reprinted by permission.

TO MY SONS

"Would you tell me, please, which way I might go from here?"

"That depends a good deal on where you want to get to," said the Cat.

> A conversation between Alice and the Cheshire Cat in *Alice's Adventures in Wonderland* by Lewis Carroll.

CONTENTS

▌NTRODUCTION

▌ assume that you are reading this book (or contemplating doing so) because you are not completely satisfied with the way things are at the present time in your life. Perhaps you see others around you with no more talents or abilities than you have and possibly even less intelligence, and yet they seem to be far ahead in collecting their share of the good things that life has to offer.

If that is true, or even only partly true, something must be going wrong and you must do something to correct it. The fact that you are reading these lines is an excellent sign that you are ready to take action against whatever it is that has been holding you back, and that alone indicates that you are likely to succeed. The question is whether this particular book can show you what course to take and how to steer yourself to whatever it is you want. I believe it can and I will tell you why.

As the publisher, editor, and reader of hundreds of

the greatest so-called "inspirational" books, I know what they all boil down to, what their basic precepts are, and what their recipes and remedies are for the human condition. Most of the books say the same things but in different words, often from different angles. For example, I published two golf instruction books some years ago, one entitled *The Nine Bad Shots of Golf* and the other, *The Four Magic Moves to Winning Golf*. If you were to follow the instructions in either book you would end up doing the same things. Some people learned a lot from the first book and claimed to have gotten nothing out of the other, while other readers reacted in the opposite way. The angle from which a subject is taught can have different effects on different people. The vocabulary that is used is equally important. As with the golf books, I found the same dichotomy of reactions to the inspirational books I published—some people swore by one and didn't take to another, although they both led you to the same place philosophically speaking.

With this in mind, I have collected the essential principles of the best inspirational books and presented them from various angles, using different words to illustrate the same basic principles so that if you don't understand them in one context, you will in another. That is also one reason why I recommend that you read it through once quickly and then reread it. You will find that a second reading of some of the principles will have greater meaning once you have seen the entire picture. It is as though you were doing a jigsaw puzzle and didn't know what the end result was supposed to be. At first you pick up a white piece, then a few yellow pieces, then some blue. After a while you realize you will be completing the picture of a sailboat in the water on a bright sunny day. Now, well before you have completed the picture, you have a good idea where every piece left over should fit. The second time you do the puzzle you'll know where everything fits right at the start. Your second reading of some parts (if not all) of this book will have the same effect. Each principle will be smoothly and appropriately interlocked with the other knowledge in your subconscious. Once there, it will work for you the way a miracle chip programs a computer to come up with the right answers.

As far as the title of this book is concerned, I would like to explain its derivation.

The principles outlined in this book react with each other in the same way that the individual players on a team depend on each other. Once you have become aware of what those principles are, you will be amazed to see how easily you can put them into practice in your daily life. You won't have to think about them: it will become second nature to you.

After having read the numerous inspirational books I referred to, I asked myself if there was any one element— any one underlying point—that was common to them all. The answer, I believe, is yes: there is one such factor that if not expressed is implicit in every book I have read on this subject. It is the assumption that the reader knows what it is that he or she wants. Yet, that is precisely what most people do not really know. As Charles Caleb Colton, the nineteenth-century English poet, said, "We are ruined, not by what we really want, but by what we *think* we do." *You cannot get what you want unless you know what you want.* George Bernard Shaw said that, "Anyone who doesn't know what he wants will have to be satisfied with what he gets." And that seems to be the plight of most people. It hung me up for years; but the moment I knew exactly where and how I wanted to live, I began to get all the specific things I wished for.

Thus, *knowing what you want* is where the ball park is. Not until you get there are you ready to take your turn at bat; I mean ready to apply the principles that you were told would enable you to achieve your aims. This belief of mine was reinforced when I came across a passage in a

Time magazine cover story about the actor Paul Newman. It told that he had no regrets, that maybe he wished he were actor Laurence Olivier or auto racer Mario Andretti, "but I guess I don't wish it hard enough or fiercely enough." And then it hit me! Paul Newman's use of the word *wish* led me to the end of my search for a title.

It seemed clear from what Newman said that because he knew what he wanted, he managed to get as much of it as he was motivated to wish for. Before you can make a wish you obviously have to know what it is that you desire. Once you know what you want—not what you *think* you want—you will get it.

Your mind is a much better computer than any that man has ever constructed. All you have to do is give it the right program and you will get the right result. Each time you consciously reflect on what it is that you desire, you are providing your "computer" with a miracle chip.

The key, then, is knowing what you want. You will then be programmed to reach your goal just as surely as a missile has been guided to reach its destination.

My search for a title was over:

Know What You Want—and Get It!

1

Can
A BOOK REALLY
CHANGE YOUR LIFE?

At the outset I would like to convince you that a meaningful book, thoughtfully read, can actually change your life dramatically. By *change* I mean produce the following effects:

- —Program your mind (the way a computer is programmed) so that you consciously and subconsciously take those steps that will lead you to get what you want out of life.
- —Steer your course (as though you were a guided missile) so that you reach your destination no matter what.
- —Lead you from frustration and disappointment to fulfillment and success.

That is exactly what certain books have done for me. To be specific, it was the principles I learned from my reading that enabled me to get bigger and better jobs, to get my own books and songs published, to invent a best-selling word game, and to found Cornerstone Library, a book publishing company that is now a highly profitable division of Simon & Schuster, Inc. The same principles that worked for me can without a doubt work for you. Although I can illustrate those principles so that you will know exactly what to do to make your wishes come true, it will be up to you to *think* about them and *apply* them in your daily life.

First I would like to tell you how I happened to read the first book that changed my life overnight. The title was *How to Attract Good Luck and Make the Most of It in Your Daily Life.* Even though the author, A. H. Z. Carr, was an adviser to Presidents Franklin D. Roosevelt and Harry Truman, I would ordinarily have scoffed at the idea of reading such a book. You would have had to pay me to read works such as *The Magic of Believing, The Magic of Thinking Big, How I Raised Myself from Failure to Success,* etc. They sounded like banal bromides written for solely commercial purposes—books that had nothing new to say except what anybody with a little common sense already knew. However, *How to Attract Good Luck* was about to be published by Simon and Schuster, where I had a relatively menial job. My job at that time included chauffeuring Richard L. Simon, the cofounder, to and from the office.

Dick Simon was a very outgoing person who used to discuss his business matters with me while we were driving together. My secret wish was that someday I would impress him by coming up with a great idea to help solve one of his problems. As it turned out, he was having a problem finding the right advertising approach in launching *How to Attract Good Luck,* so I thought I'd read it and see if I might have a good suggestion.

Thank God I read it! By applying one of its principles immediately I began a collaboration with Walt Kelly on *Songs of the Pogo,* a best-selling book as well as a highly successful record album. In the fourth chapter I will outline the principles of *How to Attract Good Luck* for you and show you exactly how it led to the Walt Kelly collaboration. Before that I want to continue with the theme of this chapter: to convince you that books do change people's lives.

About ten years ago, when I had already founded Cornerstone Library, I came across an interesting story in the newspapers. It was about Warren Grimes, a millionaire, who said he owed all of his success to the principles he learned from a book called *Working with God* by Gardner Hunting. Mr. Grimes said that up to the age of thirty-five he had accomplished very little in life. Then he happened to read this paragraph from *Working with God*:

"You have heard it said a thousand times that 'you can't get something for nothing.' You may or may not think that you believe this to be true, but it is true, whether you believe it or not, and everybody deep down in his inner nature knows it is true. That's why he is shy of any promise that promises too much. That's why you are probably skeptical of this little piece of print. But just let this idea get a foothold in your mind: If it is a law that I cannot get something for nothing, then it must be true of this law, as it is of all genuine laws, that it works both ways; it must be true that *I cannot give anything without getting something for it.* Ever think of that?"

Well, Warren Grimes hadn't thought of that up to that time but he never forgot it since! He started giving of himself every which way possible—his time, his energy, what little money he had—and it all started coming back to him in spades. Within three years he owned a company that manufactured equipment for airplanes and earned enough money to buy himself a private island off the coast of southeastern Florida.

I don't think I waited more than five minutes after reading the Warren Grimes story to track down a copy of *Working with God.* I then made an arrangement with the original publisher for me to bring out a paperback edition under the Cornerstone Library imprint. Incidentally, we did not have to pay the author any royalties for the rights because, guess what, he wanted to give them away free!

Shortly after publishing the paperback edition of *Working with God,* I noticed that the *Reader's Digest* did a series called, "Try Giving Yourself Away", based on essentially the same principles that Gardner Hunting espoused. I don't mean to imply that the *Reader's Digest* series was imitative in any way, and for all I know may have preceded Hunting's book. The point is that the underlying philosophy of giving, as opposed to taking, has high credibility.

The time-honored expression "It is better to give than to receive" often is said in jest, but its longevity is ample testimony of its substance. While the merits of giving have

5

been espoused for years, especially in Sunday sermons, *Working with God* is the only book I know that offers a Newtonian "material law" as proof of the powerful effects of giving—namely, that every action of *giving* leads to an equal and opposite reaction of *getting*.

Another book that changed people's lives, including my own, was *The Magic of Believing* by Claude Bristol. When I published the paperback edition of that book I had heard that Phyllis Diller attributed her success to its contents. I called her and asked if she would be willing to give us a quote for the front cover of our edition. This is what she wrote: "*The Magic of Believing* changed my life. Read it and . . . any problem can be solved, happiness can be achieved, great rewards can be reaped."

Liberace, the great entertainer, was another reader of *The Magic of Believing* who attributed his success to his having read the book. From time to time he would appear on talk shows—Johnny Carson, Merv Griffin, etc.—and he would acknowledge the fact that his life was changed by reading *The Magic of Believing*. Sales of the book would zoom as a result, and I wonder how many readers, because of Liberace and Phyllis Diller, have dramatic stories to tell!

I made it a point to publish (or *reprint* in paperback editions) as many as I could of the books that influenced me. In the course of publishing a book many people are involved in the preliminary process—the typesetter, the proofreader, the cover designer, etc., all of whom have to read either a part or all of the book. One of my greatest sources of satisfaction used to occur when one of those people would tell me how the particular book in question changed his or her life for the better. Many of the people who worked for me were inspired to attain new levels of achievement because it was their job to read what we used to call personal guides, or inspirational books. My dear friend Terry Garrity, later famous as "J," was motivated to write one of the greatest best sellers of all time—*The Sensuous Woman*—partially as a result of being involved in the publicity and promotion of our inspirational books.

Am I convincing you that a book can do wonders for you? That this very book you are now reading can do what I have been describing up to now? Or are you saying that my examples relate to people who had special talents that would have become manifest sooner or later? If the latter, then be prepared to change your mind. I could regale you with stories of very ordinary people with no special talents who have achieved storybook successes through the "storybooks" that I have mentioned. But right now it wouldn't be worth your while to read a list of repetitious case histories. Read on with an open mind, and I am sure that before you have reached the last page you will have experienced tangible proof of what I have been trying to tell you. Nothing would give me greater satisfaction than to learn of this.

Dorothea Brande, the author of *Wake Up and Live!*, told how reading one particular sentence in a book changed the whole course of her life. Here is part of her introduction to *Wake Up and Live!* in which she tells of that remarkable experience:

"Two years ago I came across a formula for success which has revolutionized my life. It was so simple, and so obvious once I had seen it, that I could hardly believe it was responsible for the magical results which followed my putting it into practice.

"The first thing to confess is that two years ago I was a failure. Oh, nobody knew it except me and those who knew me well enough to see that I was doing a tenth of what could be expected of me. I held an interesting position, lived not too dull a life—yet there was no doubt, in my own mind, at least, that I had failed. What I was doing was a substitute activity for what I had planned to do; and no matter how ingenious and neat the theories were

7

which I presented to myself to account for my lack of success, I knew very well that there was more work that I should be doing, and better work, and work more demonstrably my own.

"Of course, I was always looking for a way out of my impasse. But when I actually had the good fortune to find it, I hardly believed in my own luck. . . .

"For I had been years in my deadlock; I had known what I wanted to do, had equipped myself for my profession—and got nowhere. Yet I had chosen my life-work, which was writing, early, and had started out with high hopes. Most of the work I had finished had met a friendly reception. But then when I tried to take the next step and go on to a more mature phase, it was as though I had been turned to stone. I felt as if I could not start.

"Of course it goes without saying that I was unhappy . . . . I busied myself at editing, since I seemed doomed to fail at the more creative side of literature; and I never ceased harrying myself, consulting teachers and analysts and psychologists and physicians for advice as to how to get out of my pit. . . . I tried every suggestion for relief. Nothing worked more than temporarily. For a while I might engage in feverish activity, but never for more than a week or two. Then the period of action would suddenly end, leaving me as far from my goal as ever, and each time more deeply discouraged.

"Then, between one minute and the next, I found the idea which set me free. This time I was not consciously looking for it; . . . But I came across a sentence in the book I was reading: *Human Personality,* by F. W. H. Myers, which was so illuminating that I put the book aside to consider all the ideas suggested in that one penetrating hypothesis. When I picked up the book again I was a different person."

In a later chapter I will of course discuss the sentence

that so profoundly affected Dorothea Brande.* I will also reveal the conclusions that she came to about why so many of us fail to use our abilities to the full—why we don't get so many of the things we desire, despite the fact that we are fully capable of doing so. For now, I hope you are ready to believe that what happened to me, to Dorothea Brande, and to so many others through books will definitely happen to you.

So far I have been referring to so-called inspirational books, books whose major theme is about the road to success and happiness. However, I have come across many other kinds of books that had nothing to do with self-improvement but which contained profound insights into human behavior. For example, a book on how to write a play, by John van Druten, taught me a principle that I used over and over in writing advertising copy; an introduction to a book on humor taught me how to educate myself on any new subject; a book about dealing with children taught me an invaluable lesson about how to deal with adults. I will discuss these books in chapter 7 and spell out the simple, yet profound, principles involved. For now I just want to impress on you that any number of worthwhile books on a variety of subjects can affect your life *if you are alert to the fact that they have that potential.* Once you are convinced, your antennae will begin to pick up all sorts of messages that you otherwise might have missed.

But what does all this have to do with our subject? Does a book by a playwright on playwriting relate to getting what you want? Or one by a child psychologist on dealing with children?

The answer is a very definite yes. Philosophical principles that favorably affect your behavior must help you

* See pages 84-85.

get what you want. Such principles of behavior are often espoused in the least likely places. I have found them in cookbooks as well as books on philosophy or psychology. The essential thing is to be aware that this is true.

Perhaps I have belabored this point, but I did so because in my own experience I missed a great many "messages" by not being alert to the possibility of their presence in a particular situation. Being receptive, having an open mind, therefore, is the first step of the journey to the magical results of making serious, thoughtful wishes for the things we want out of life.

I now want to elaborate on the other first steps we need to consider.

2

FIRST STEPS IN FULFILLING YOUR DESIRES

Just as I was preparing to write this chapter I came across an article in the February 7, 1983, issue of *Time* magazine entitled "Make a Wish." It tells how communities from Baltimore, Maryland, to Oregon City, Oregon, are now publishing "wish lists" of services and items they want but cannot afford. "In many cities, the lists are dominated by pleas for park and sports equipment. Others want typewriters and computers for city offices, film projectors and pianos for community centers."

The result?

Local citizens are making donations that are paying for the costs of those services and items, a dramatic demonstration of the fact that if a community knows what it wants, it gets what it wants—its wishes come true.

What is true about communities and cities holds equally true for you: before you can *get* what you want, you have to *know* what you want. This sounds simple, but it really isn't. To know what you want takes a great deal of self-analysis and effort. Most people only *think* they know what they want. Often, after striving for a lifetime to get certain things, people find that what they have gotten isn't what they really wanted after all.

The question is: how can you know you really want something before you actually get it? The truth is that you cannot be absolutely certain in advance but you owe it to yourself to do a little thinking and research.

For example, suppose you never lived in a house in the suburbs but think that is what you would like. How do you know before you move out of the city and into the suburbs? Well, obviously there are certain things you can do to check your feelings before making a major commitment. For instance, you might rent a suburban house for a week or a month. Although people generally check things out carefully before buying a home or a car, they are incredibly lax when it comes to some of the most important things in life.

If a fairy godmother asked you to specify your wishes so that she could make them come true, would you be able to tell her, for example,

1. What kind of work you would enjoy doing?
2. Where you would like to live?
3. What friends you would like to have that you don't have now?
4. What causes you would help promote?
5. What subjects you would like to learn or know more about?
6. What an ideal day, or week, or month in your life would entail from morning till night?

These questions seem so obvious that you may not be raising them consciously, or you may feel that it is frustrating to raise them because you think you can't do anything about them anyway. But if you are to get what you want, you must try to specify what you want, no matter how unattainable your desires may now seem.

You might find it interesting to ask some of your friends these questions and see how specifically they can answer them. You also may be surprised to find how many people have difficulty in giving the answers.

The more questions you ask yourself about your wishes, the better you will be able to define them; the better you define them, the greater are the chances of their coming true. However, if you say there is no use thinking about wishes because there's nothing you can do to fulfill them, you will be right—you can't do anything constructive if you believe you can't. Just as you can make your own luck (as I will demonstrate in chapter 4), you can make your own truth. The magic of nonbelieving is just as effective as the magic of believing. With a positive outlook, however, you can make positive truths, i.e., the fulfillment of your desires. At the very least you will be moving in the right direction instead of drifting.

Drifting. . . . That word brings a lot to mind about my own life. I think of how many years I was like a detached leaf moving wherever the wind happened to blow me. It didn't occur to me that I could control my own direction against outside random forces. However, just as a sailboat can get to its destination no matter which way the wind is blowing, so can a human being reach a given destination despite forces that may seem to be opposed.*

Blind acceptance of things the way they are (existing circumstances) is the easy way out, and that is why so many of us stay in a rut. The more you question the validity of your present circumstances, the more likely you are to do something about improving them. Creativity is nothing more than the art of rearranging things that already exist, whether they be different combinations of colors, notes in the scale, or parts of an automobile. The motivation for rearranging things—becoming creative—is a dissatisfaction with the status quo, or things the way they are. The basic cause of all dissatisfaction is a wish for something other than what is there.

Analytical and perceptive wishing as a result of knowing what you want is the final step in changing the status quo in your life. To have a rational wishful thought requires self-analysis, as well as some questioning of your present desires and aims. The mere act of doing this will provide a momentum in your life that will propel you toward your goals, whatever they may be.

The great German poet Goethe put it this way:

"I respect the man who knows distinctly what he

*As a matter of fact, opposing forces can often be used to supply the power for getting what you want! I will discuss this further in chapter 6, "Mental Judo: Putting the Intellectual Strength of Others to Your Own Use."

wishes. The greater part of all the mischief in the world arises from the fact that men do not sufficiently understand their own aims. They have undertaken to build a tower, and spent no more labor on the foundation than would be necesary to erect a hut."

As I said before, to get what you want you have to know what you want. To know what you want, you have to try doing new things and meeting new people. For example, if your life depended on it, do you think you could:

1. Make up an interesting story?
2. Write a poem?
3. Paint a picture of a piece of fruit on a table?
4. Make up your own recipe for a tasty dish?
5. Act a part in a play?
6. Make an interesting object out of a piece of clay?

Could you do any one of these things *if your life depended on it*? If the answer is yes and you have never tried these things, maybe your life does depend on it! Maybe you will discover a hidden talent, or a better-than-average ability to do a certain thing. Maybe you will learn to know what you want. At the very least you will be doing something different. That in itself is a virtue the importance of which cannot be exaggerated.

Winston Churchill said that he never really noticed many different shades of colors until he took up oil painting and tried to paint scenes from his garden. Then, he suddenly became aware of a whole new world of color that he had ignored for the previous forty years of his life.

There are worlds of experience at your fingertips that you may be ignoring and are therefore depriving yourself of the joy of living. You will never know what you want unless you try new things. If you are happy and fulfilled the way things are, then you should just keep doing what you are doing. But if you sense a lack of fulfillment, a feeling that you're missing out on things that others seem to have, then your first priority must be to seek a new venture—an *ad*venture, if you will.

The best summary of what I have been trying to say in this chapter may be found in the words of two different English poets, Robert Southwell and Joseph Hall. The first said, "To a resolute mind, wishing to do is the first step toward doing." Joseph Hall said that "Our wishes are the true touchstone of our estate; such as we wish to be we are . . . We cannot better know what we are than by what we would be."

I can think of no better way to end this chapter than by asking you to reflect on the words I have just quoted. If you do, and if you try to apply them to your everyday life, you will have taken a giant step toward making your dreams come true.

3

LEARNING TO KNOW WHAT YOU REALLY WANT

At one time in his life Benjamin Franklin decided to try to lead a life of moral perfection. He deeply believed that virtue was its own reward and that no qualities were so likely to make a poor man's fortune as those of probity and integrity. These are the virtues that he decided to live up to in accordance with his own definitions of them:

1. **Temperance**—Eat not to dullness; drink not to elevation.
2. **Silence**—Speak not but what may benefit others or yourself; avoid trifling conversation.
3. **Order**—Let all your things have their places; let each part of your business have its time.
4. **Resolution**—Resolve to perform what you ought; perform without fail what you resolve.
5. **Frugality**—Make no expense but to do good to others or yourself; i.e., waste nothing.
6. **Industry**—Lose no time; be always employ'd in something useful; cut off all unnecessary actions.
7. **Sincerity**—Use no hurtful deceit; think innocently and justly, and, if you speak, speak accordingly.
8. **Justice**—Wrong none by doing injuries or omitting benefits that are your duty.
9. **Moderation**—Avoid extremes; forbear resenting injuries so much as you think they deserve.
10. **Cleanliness**—Tolerate no uncleanliness in body, clothes, or habitation.
11. **Tranquillity**—Be not disturbed at trifles, or at accidents common or unavoidable.
12. **Chastity**—Rarely use venery but for health or offspring, never to dullness, weakness, or the injury of your own or another's peace or reputation.
13. **Humility**—Imitate Jesus and Socrates.

His plan was to concentrate on one particular virtue at a time for the period of a week, but even so to try to abide by them all. He made up a little book which had a page for each virtue and he kept a daily score of his success. The score was simply to indicate by a black mark that he had committed a fault on a particular day with respect to a particular virtue.

Within a short time Benjamin Franklin realized that he had bitten off more than he could chew. As he wrote, "I was surprised to find myself so much fuller of faults than I had imagined; but I had the satisfaction of seeing them diminish." Eventually he decided not to try for absolute perfection and tells why in a humorous way. He says there was a man who wanted his ax to be as bright and polished on the whole of its surface as it was on its edge. Therefore, he put it to the grindstone (with the help of a smith), and when the effort seemed to be exhausting, decided to leave the ax as it then was. The smith, who had the easy part of the job, was willing to continue helping with the grinding, saying, "Turn on, turn on; we shall have it bright by-and-by; as yet it is only speckled." "Yes," said the man, *"but I think I like a speckled ax best."* In the same way, Ben Franklin told himself that "a perfect character might be attended with the inconvenience of being envied or hated;* and that a benevolent man should allow a few faults in himself to keep his friends in countenance."

I believe that Franklin's list of virtues is an excellent one and I actually tried to see how well I could live up to it. Like the man with the ax, I decided that a somewhat "speckled" Norman Monath was preferable to a colorless one! However, I did learn something important as a result of my efforts: I learned a great deal about my sense of values, about what meant the most to me, and about what I wanted for myself. I believe that anyone who tries the experiment will find it equally rewarding and I strongly recommend it.

When discussing this chapter with my friend Strome

*See pages 82-83.

Lamon, the advertising director of Simon and Schuster, he suggested the following exercise: on any given day, choose to examine some of your actions and question whether they match your ideals. For example, if you are awakened by an alarm clock, is that the kind of alarm that suits you best? Is the toothbrush you are using, or the bath towel, exactly what you would now choose if you *had* to make the best choice? This exercise, of course, ties in beautifully with the ideas of challenging our assumptions and reassessing our prerogatives.* But in addition, it raises our consciousness with respect to what we really want.

Marjorie Novak, like Strome Lamon, is someone to whom I will always be grateful for supporting me at a time when I needed it most. That was the time when I was in the bookkeeping department and she was my supervisor. In those days we were not allowed to leave the office unless our accounts were in balance, and there were numerous times when mine would be out by a few cents, or thousands of dollars. (It didn't matter which as far as being able to leave was concerned.) Marjorie always showed me how to find my errors and saved me hours of needless trial-and-error operations. Eventually she became executive vice-president of a small but growing publishing company until her retirement as a very wealthy and happy woman. If I had to name one factor above all others that was responsible for her success, it would not be her ingenuity in finding bookkeeping errors. It would be something she did that helped her a great deal in learning what she really wanted.

She used to keep a diary of the various discussions she had with the other executives in the course of business meetings, luncheons, and conferences. The value in keeping those records was not so much in recalling what

*See chapter 7.

the other people said, but in being able to remember her *own* thought processes at the time.

In the first place, it doesn't take many notes (after a meeting has taken place) to put down the essentials of what was discussed and the thrust of what each individual did. It is amazing how much your mind will recall when reminded of just a few details. Once, during a trip through France, I jotted down a sentence or two each night recalling one scene or event that would "describe" the day, so to speak. Years later when I would refer to those short sentences, I would instantly recall minute details of all else that happened on those days. So it doesn't take many notes to serve as an effective reminder. Secondly, it follows that from just few short notes you will recall much about your thought processes at a particular time, and the ability to do this is of immense value in delineating your motivations, your innermost desires, your deepest wishes.

It is difficult in the abstract to try to recall what we thought we wanted at certain times in our life, but whenever we can do so, it does so much for our ability to understand the present. Knowing where we came from tells us where we are. Only when we know where we are can we go to where we want to be. And that is why I am never surprised to learn how many successful people have taken notes, kept diaries, or made some kinds of recordings of events in their lives to which they could refer from time to time, the way Marjorie Novak did.

More often than you may realize, you will be surprised at what your line of thinking was at a particular time. This is healthy, since changes in your thinking reflect experience and growth. However, it is essential to know exactly how you have changed and this you can do only by keeping some sort of record. Businessmen often have to refer to their previous correspondence and memoranda; doing this has some of the beneficial effects of what might be called "mental review." Statesmen and others elected to high office often write books about their experiences and so are also forced into this process. In the event that your particular occupation does not have such a built-in feature, I urge you to keep a diary of sorts. It doesn't have to be elaborate or detailed. Just a sentence or two will suffice to spark your memory to a surprising degree.

Another exercise in learning what we want is suggested by something David Seabury wrote in *The Art of Selfishness*. In the chapter "Know Your Own Mind," he asks that you do the following: "Try the law of economy on your personality. Boil yourself down to a few attributes you are certain are characteristic of your nature. Accent those phases. Insist on being true to them. Don't compromise them on any occasion. From this start in personal integrity, you will soon get to know yourself."

Obviously, the more you get to know yourself through this test of your personal integrity, the more you will learn what your true desires are.

Perhaps you have heard it said that if you can't get what you want, you should learn to want what you get. However, that sort of negative approach is shattered by David Schwartz throughout *The Magic of Thinking Big* and I couldn't agree more. The only time to "settle" for what you have is when what you have is what you want. That is the only way to make progress.

A knowledge of basic psychology can be extremely useful in giving us insights into our psyches so that we can learn our true needs. Anne Miller, a friend of mine, was a mother of five children when she started studying psychology on her own. From this she learned that she wanted to become a lawyer, and did so. Today she is a full partner in a very successful law firm that specializes in criminal law, and her friends continue to be amazed at her accomplishment. They thought Anne was doomed to remain in the kitchen for the foreseeable future, particularly since the children were small when she started law school. However, once she knew what she wanted, she was able to get her husband's full cooperation in helping out domestically so that she was able to become a law student without neglecting the needs of the children.

Of course, anyone who has undergone psychoanalysis or psychotherapy with good results must certainly have been made aware of his or her basic wishes. However, if you did not have that experience, I believe that if you were to read a few basic books on psychology you would find them just as helpful as my friend Anne Miller did.

Another subject that is worth looking into is the interpretation of our dreams. In the song entitled "Wishing Will Make It So" by B. G. de Silva, we are told that the wishes we make while we're awake are the equivalent of the dreams we dream while we're asleep. Dreams are very often the wishes we wish while we're asleep, and a knowledge of their meaning can unlock many doors in our search for self-knowledge.

If you have difficulty in interpreting your dreams, you might ask a close friend to help you. It may be easier for someone who knows you fairly well to arrive at the true meaning of your dreams because you may be repressing what you may not want to face about yourself. Dreams are a convenient way to express whatever we may be trying to hide from ourselves, so we sometimes concoct scenarios that seem to defy analysis. We do this mainly in order to protect ourselves from feelings of guilt or anxiety. However, some of our close friends may not be fooled by the symbols we use in our dreams and may be surprisingly accurate in explaining what they mean.

One of the clearest explanations of what dreams are is in *The Meaning of Your Dreams* by a dear friend of mine, Valerie Moolman. Valerie says:

"The format of the dream is necessarily a little different from that of the waking-thought. With the conscious mind turned off, our use of language is restricted. We dream-think non-verbally, for the most part, which restricts both the presentation and the subject matter. Instead of articulating words, we see pictures. Instead of becoming aware of concepts or abstractions entering our heads, we see shapes symbolic of those thoughts appearing as if on a screen in front of us or on a stage around us. If an idea is incapable of presentation in this manner, with perhaps a little assist from sound or emotional coloring, we simply don't dream about it.

"The pictures we see represent our thoughts; the symbols (in the form of people, creatures, houses, objects and so on) are representations of our abstract ideas or conceptions. Each dreamer creates his own story, plots it and peoples it; the emotions in it are his emotions. The actions, characters, feelings, colors, shadings, are all put there by him and *only* by him, although he will often call upon the most casual experiences of the day to shape the dream-stuff of the night. Even the least imaginative of us may have dreams that seem to be bizarre, yet are not. They have a superficial weirdness because we cannot readily untangle the symbolism and find out what it is that we are talking to ourselves about at night. The night thoughts are really hidden daytime thoughts brought out of hiding by our sleeping minds—and yet not brought *altogether* out of hiding or the shock of recognition might awaken us.

"The thoughts that occupy us are not mere trivia, either. We do not dream of things for which we have absolutely no concern; we dream of deeply rooted problems, of secret wishes that demand fulfillment, or conflicts that matter to us very much. Even when a dream appears ridiculous—*particularly* then—it is a representation of something that is troubling us. Neither does it come simply to annoy; it parades the facts before our eyes and quite often offers solutions to the very problems it presents."

From time to time people tell me to stop dreaming and wake up to reality. The truth is that very often my dreaming *is* the reality, whereas the so-called reality is nothing more than an act—an act of going through whatever emotions I feel will help me accommodate to the pressures of society. In other words, the reality is a sham—an act of hypocrisy—while the dream is an expression of my true self, my true longings, my innermost wishes. The point is this: there may be times when it is kinder and more humane to play a part than to use truth as though it were a deadly weapon. However, when we do shade the truth, we must be sure we are fully aware that we are doing so. Otherwise, there is a danger that we might end up deluding ourselves and become confused about what we want out of life.

You've heard the expression "Beauty is in the eye of the beholder." Whenever I hear it, I always think of how difficult it is to see things as they are instead of as we wish they were. In personal relationships, this can cause serious problems. For example, suppose you have an image in mind of the kind of person you want for a companion, or lover, or spouse. Let's say that there are five or six attributes that are especially important for that person to have in order to measure up to your ideal. One attribute might be a love for classical music, or golf, or horseback riding; another might be a certain kind of taste in clothes or food, etc. Now, along comes someone who has three of the five or six attributes you are seeking. Instead of recognizing that, you bestow *all* the remaining attributes on that person; you are so eager to find your "ideal" that you prematurely end the search by hypnotizing yourself into thinking you have found all that you wanted. The result is that six months or a year later you wake up and say, "What did I ever see in him/her?" The answer: you saw what you were looking for—what you wanted to see—not what was really there.

In the same way that we can delude ourselves about people through our impatience, anxiety, or overpowering inner longings, we can fool ourselves into thinking we have what we want in other areas—the job we have, the house or apartment we live in, the part of the country we live in, etc. While we may be temporarily content in this act of self-delusion, eventually we find that a feeling of malaise begins to appear and starts escalating into deep unhappiness.

How do we prevent this from happening to us? Once again, by testing ourselves as to our preferences in dealing with the minutiae in our lives. It is those seemingly minor matters that get us into the habit of taking things for granted and getting into a rut. But once we question whether we like the sound of our doorbell, for instance, we are on the road to examining our options in matters of greater significance.

Another very important habit we must develop, if we are to know what we want, is to try to live in the present instead of the past or the future. That may sound strange at first, but if you think about it, you may agree that it makes sense. When I first came across that idea, I began to notice how many of us live in either a state of reminiscence or a state of anticipation about the future, instead of being fully conscious of the present, the moment at hand. Reminiscence and anticipation can be very important components in bringing satisfaction and happiness into our lives, but overemphasizing either, or both, brings about an unfortunate result: we end up wondering why time seemed to fly by too quickly for us to have done what we wanted to do; we end up with a feeling that life has passed us by. On the other hand, if we continually impress ourselves that the *present*—the *moment* of consciousness—is the most important moment in our lives, we won't let it slip by carelessly but we will savor it for what it is worth and for how we might take advantage of it. "Seize the day" is a well-known expression, but the best preparation for doing that is to get into the habit of seizing the moment at hand.

The next time you find yourself spending fifteen to thirty or so minutes with someone, ask yourself how much of that time you spent thinking about things that had already happened, or were going to happen later on. I am not referring to actual conversations *about* the past or future. For example, if the other person asked what you ate for breakfast the day before, your answer will involve the past although your mind can be concentrated on the conversation taking place. I am referring to a situation where you may be having a conversation about the weather, or your job, and while it is going on, somewhere in the back of your head you are thinking about an incident that took place a day or two before, or you are thinking about the date you are looking forward to the following week. You are not really focused on the moment at hand, the *present* moment, and that can lead to trouble.

Of course, you will always have fleeting thoughts about the past and future—you have to as a person of intelligence with a memory and with hopes. However, there is a difference between holding the present in perspective against the *background* of the past and future as opposed to blurring the present because the past and future preoccupations are allowed to intrude. And it is amazing to what extent we do that. We end up missing the experience of the present and before we know it, the years go by.

The present should be treasured. This is the moment you have been living for all your life. Now, while you are reading these lines, is the time you should ask yourself: Am I doing what I want to? Am I happy? Am I what I wanted to grow up to be when I was a child? If you cannot give positive answers to those questions now, what makes you think you will be able to do so later on? Perhaps there is a good reason, but you had better search for it right away if you don't know it now.

As an exercise, try to treat each moment of the present as though it is the moment you had been waiting for all your life. As a matter of fact, it *is*. When you have raised your consciousness along these lines, you will regard each moment as though it were a precious jewel to be guarded with your life. Then, you will find yourself listening better, seeing more clearly, living a life of greater satisfaction and gratification, even through periods of grief. For then you will be controlling your thoughts, learning what it is you really want, taking your life in hand and wishing for the right things at the right time and with the right intensity.

Now, as I promised earlier, I will outline the principles of attracting good luck.

4

THE PRINCIPLES OF ATTRACTING GOOD LUCK

Attracting good luck depends on chance to some degree but not totally. If chance alone were the activating factor, then it would take voodooism or some other form of black magic to bring about lucky situations, opportunities, and results. However, just as a skilled poker player can increase his or her chances of winning a pot by following certain principles, you can increase your chances of "winning" good fortune by doing certain specific things.

We are constantly subject to acts of chance over which we have no control. Some chances can lead to disaster, some can lead to success. We must make it our business to expose ourselves to the kinds of chances that lead to success. If you wanted to expose yourself to bad luck, you would certainly know how to do it. You could even arrange to get struck by lightning if you were determined to do so. Just stay on golf courses during thunderstorms, with an iron in your hand, and sooner or later you'll be struck. (According to golf pro Lee Trevino, however, you shouldn't use a 1-iron because even God can't hit one!) Getting struck by good luck instead of lightning can also be arranged by the correct exposure. That then is the first principle.

PRINCIPLES OF ATTRACTING GOOD LUCK

1. Exposure

2.

3.

According to Albert Carr, the author of *How to Attract Good Luck*, the best exposure to the kinds of chances that lead to good luck is in meeting new people whose interests may be relevant to your own. I'll give you an example from my own experience.

In the last chapter I said that I started to read Albert Carr's book because of Dick Simon. A few days after I read it, Walt Kelly happened to visit the offices of Simon and Schuster and as usual the company rolled out the red carpet for him. His Pogo cartoon strip was widely syndicated and his books were national best sellers. I used to wish that I could meet him, but that didn't seem likely, given my menial position with the firm. However, on this particular visit Walt Kelly had a question about music that his editor was unable to answer and so his editor posed the question to me over the phone. (I used to supplement my income by playing cocktail piano at private parties in those days, and so people in the office thought I knew something about music.) Walt's question related to doing some musical research, and I quickly told his editor what sources were available. Then I hung up the phone.

About thirty seconds after hanging up, it struck me that here was a chance to meet Walt Kelly—a chance to put into practice the first principle I had learned from *How to Attract Good Luck*. With great trepidation, I called Kelly's editor and volunteered to do the research for Mr. Kelly if he so desired. The result was that Walt Kelly invited me for a drink after work, which began a relationship that led to our collaboration on a book and record album. Thus my wish was fulfilled when I simply exposed myself to a chance to attract good luck.

For once in my life I attracted good luck *consciously*. First I began with a *wish* to meet a specific person, Walt Kelly. I knew what I wanted. Second, I was alert to the possibility of meeting him by offering my free services, giving of myself. Third was the inevitable result of the first two steps: a meeting that resulted in further meetings where we could discuss our mutual interests and end up combining them to our mutual advantage.

Here is another example of the exposure principle. Francine Prince had written *The Dieter's Gourmet Cook-*

book and was hoping to build a career as an author in the field of nutrition. Well, she really knew what she wanted, but she needed a lucky break. It came through an invitation to a party which she accepted because I told her that Bill Adler would be there. Bill Adler is one of the foremost literary agents (as well as a best-selling author) in the business, representing such clients as Mike Wallace, Phil Donahue, Dan Rather, Ronald and Nancy Reagan, etc. When Francine expressed her wish to Bill about furthering her career, he immediately came up with the concept and title of *Diet for Life*, one of the best-selling diet books in the country. That was good luck for both of them, they having used the exposure principle to fulfill an inner wish.

Besides *exposure* there are two other factors that must come into play in order to bring about good luck. They are the principles of *recognition* and *response*.

PRINCIPLES OF ATTRACTING GOOD LUCK

1. Exposure

2. Recognition

3. Response

Once you have exposed yourself to the proper chances you must be able to *recognize* when a particular situation presents a real opportunity. And once recognized, you must *respond* properly. For example, after I had successfully arranged to meet Walt Kelly it might have developed that I simply did some research for him. However, my reading of *How to Attract Good Luck* indicated that an opportunity was lurking here and I didn't want to miss it. From that book I knew I had to *respond* in some productive way to my having met Kelly and so my mind was working overtime as we were having our drinks. Then it occurred to me! He was writing books, I was writing songs—why not collaborate? Instead of making that suggestion on the spot, I decided just to go ahead and set one of his cartoon-strip lyrics to a tune that I would compose. My creative response proved to be very lucky because Walt loved my setting of "Don't Sugar Me!," which became one of our most popular songs.

Exposure, Recognition, and Response, then, are the three elements involved in attracting good luck according to Albert Carr. However, this gives rise to a key question: what kind of person is it who takes the trouble to put them into practice?

It isn't enough to know about principles: they work only when applied and you will apply them only when you are motivated to do so. The source of that motivation is nothing more than plain, ordinary but habitual wishing.

Of the thousands of people who have read How to Attract Good Luck, perhaps no more than ten or fifteen percent reacted to it the way I did. Many simply learned the principles but did not take the trouble to put them into practice, and not because they did not want to. I believe they had not thought about the effects of wishing. They did not realize that you must think about your wishes repeatedly and even say them out loud sometimes in order to ignite the spark that will "explode" their fulfillment.

Therefore, I urge you to make thoughtful wishes (if you haven't already done so) and try to believe that they will ultimately come true. This means thinking positively,* resulting in a positive charge to all the elements

---

*Throughout this book I refer to positive thinking as being of overriding importance with respect to everything we do. It was, of course, Dr. Norman Vincent Peale who turned those words into a household phrase through the publication of his great book, The Power of Positive Thinking.

that make you the kind of person you are. (Or, if you'll forgive the pun, a positive charge to all the ions you have in the fire.) Freud (paraphrasing Shakespeare) used the expression, "The wish is father to the thought." In other words, the thought of inventing a telephone, for example, would never arise unless there first was a wish to communicate from afar. Likewise, you won't build your particular dream house unless you begin with a particular wish, one that encompasses the size, location, and structure of your dream house, if possible. That will take some thinking on your part, not just wishing.

As I pointed out before, it is not enough simply to expose yourself to opportunities; you must also respond in some way. Many people I know come up with great ideas from time to time but only a very few ever do anything about them. One close friend of mine, Anne David, is a person who not only gets good ideas, but she also makes it her business to follow through.

Some years ago Anne was telling my wife about the different kinds of volunteer services that were possible for someone who wished to make a social contribution. I heard my wife say, "Anne, you know so much about this subject you ought to write a book about it." I immediately piped up with, "And if you do, I'll publish it!"

Now, I had said that sort of thing to numerous people and none had taken me up on it. Not Anne. Six months later she handed me a manuscript which was published as *A Guide to Volunteer Services.* Anne's personal life began to expand and she went into debt counseling. Her latest book is entitled *Get Out and Stay Out of Debt!* and she is now working on a new book.

I hope I have encouraged you to follow up on any ideas you may have *even if nothing comes of it.* The mere act of doing *something* instead of *nothing* will ultimately lead to success. Also, even if your idea fails, you will have learned a lot. (My first publishing idea failed but if I hadn't pursued it, I would not have been able to try the second, which succeeded.)

Let me close this chapter with two more examples of how the book *How to Attract Good Luck* influenced my life. The first has to do with a word game I invented called Bali.

Some time ago I used to play solitaire to while away spare time, and I usually played the form known as Canfield. This is the solitaire game that involves placing the cards in numerical sequence, alternating the colors. After a while, I got tired of placing jacks on queens, nines on tens, etc., so I tried something new. I made each card represent a letter of the alphabet instead of numbers and pictures, the result being that I could spell words instead of completing numerical sequences.

It occurred to me that other people might like my game, so I discussed it with my friends. Almost without exception they tried to discourage me from investing my time and/or money in the idea. Ordinarily I might have let them influence me sufficiently to abandon my plan to try to market the game. However, I remembered a key point that the author made in *How to Attract Good Luck*. He said that friends will very often bring up the negative aspects that might relate to new ventures, and they do so in the sincere effort to try to protect you from getting hurt. But you must not let their negativity divert you from *knowing* what you want and *getting* it.

Think of your own experiences in this regard. How many times have friends said things such as "It's been done before," or "It sounds risky," or "If I were you, I'd try something else," as opposed to "Boy, what a great idea!" or "Let's be partners."

When my friends pointed out all the drawbacks of trying to develop a new game, I was prepared. I didn't let them sway me, and as a result I've earned thousands of dollars through the years. There are now Japanese, French, and German versions on the market, thanks to the author of *How to Attract Good Luck*.

From now on, when friends try to dissuade you from new ventures, don't be influenced by any sweeping generalizations. If they have specific, negative factors to call to your attention, and you feel they know what they are talking about, you might listen. But stick to your guns if it occurs to you that they are simply trying to protect you. Also, you must remember that they have nothing to lose if they discourage you. On the other hand, if they encouraged you and you did lose money, they fear that your relationship might be adversely affected.

The second (and last) example of how *How to Attract Good Luck* influenced my life had to do with the founding of Cornerstone Library, now owned by Simon & Schuster, Inc.

Among other things, I became the chess editor of Simon and Schuster, not because of my skill but because at the office I seemed to be the one most interested in the game. As a result, I was Fred Reinfeld's editor, a man who wrote more chess books than anyone else in the world. He could write one a month and they'd all be good!

He invited my wife and me to dinner and the theater to express his gratitude for my sponsorship of his manuscripts. When I told my wife about the invitation, she was hesitant. It seemed too generous a gesture on Reinfeld's part and she felt that we weren't in a financial position to reciprocate. However, I told my wife that Fred Reinfeld met every one of the criteria spelled out in *How to Attract Good Luck* that signaled exposure to good luck. He was somebody relatively new in my life, we had common interests, he knew influential people, was a zestful, productive person and certainly seemed to be a unique one. Therefore, even if my wife and I had to extend ourselves somewhat in reciprocating Reinfeld's generous gesture, I felt it might be more than worth it.

The result was that in discussing the future of book publishing at dinner, Fred Reinfeld stirred me into thinking about paperback publishing as a possibility for myself. He even offered to introduce me to David Boehm, who helped me with all I needed to know to get started. (David went on to be the American publisher of *The Guinness Book of World Records*. Need I say more about how lucky I was to have had the benefit of Dave's advice?)

From now on whenever you have the opportunity to meet new people with whom you might share interests, make every effort to do so. Don't do what I used to do before I read *How to Attract Good Luck*, which was to say any of the following:

—I'm tired right now and would rather go to sleep.
—I'm not dressed well enough—my hair is a mess.
—They probably wouldn't be interested in me, even if I were interested in them.
—I couldn't afford to hold my own in their circle.
—I'm just not in the mood to meet anybody.

Granted that there's an element of truth in all the above statements, you must not let that deprive you of the chance to make one of your wishes come true. I suggest you revise the above statements to something like the following:

—I'm tired but I could certainly be stimulated by the right person!
—I'm not dressed as well as I'd like to be, but under the circumstances who else will really care?
—If I can't think of interesting things to say, I might be able to think of some interesting questions!

In other words, turn every negative thought into a positive one and you'll be amazed by the results. By doing this you will be hastening the process of *exposure* which we said was the first principle of attracting good luck. Taking the opportunity to meet new people seems to be the best kind of exposure that leads to good luck. In recalling a lucky break you rarely hear someone say, "I happened to talk to my brother. . ." [or sister, or mother, etc.] You invariably hear something like, "I decided to accept an invitation I wasn't enthusiastic about, but I happened to meet John for the first time and that's how we ended up owning this great new business. . ." The frame of mind, therefore, that hastens good exposure is a positive one.

The kind of thinking that will enable you to fulfill the other principles of *recognition* and *response* is reflective wishing. This will help you learn what you want. Also, thinking wishfully automatically keeps you reaching for things temporarily out of your grasp. But as long as you're reaching, you'll be ready when what you want is near, and you'll be better prepared to make a successful grasp.

Read the biographies of the great achievers and you will find numerous examples of the *exposure, recognition,* and *response* sequence in their lives. Whenever you meet someone who seems to have had a significant lucky break, go over the history of that lucky break with the person and you will be amazed to find that you can learn to do that "magic" trick yourself!

5

CONTROLLING YOUR LIFE

Whatever you are doing, do your best. Even if you don't like what you are doing, do your best. It is bound to pay dividends. If you find it is impossible to do your best in any given situation, then do your best to get out of that situation. You must. It is essential to acquire the habit of making the best of everything because if you don't, your wishing will become negative. You will find yourself saying "I wish I didn't have to do this," or "I wish I weren't at this place," or "I wish I weren't with this particular person." In that case your wishing power will be dissipated, it will become associated with negative things, and the effects on your personality and productivity will be predictably dismal.

When I first started working for Simon and Schuster, I was a book packer in their shipping room. There was nothing much to like about the job, but I needed it desperately. Consequently I did my best. Those were the days of the Great Depression, and I knew that I could have been replaced at the drop of a hat if I didn't hustle.

By chance it happened that one of the office boys at the executive offices of the company was out sick and I was sent over as a temporary replacement. I was chosen because my shipping-room boss was impressed by my hard work and he knew it was important for his own reputation to send a conscientious worker to the executive office.

When I reported to the man in charge of the mailroom at the executive office, I felt as though I had climbed Mount Everest. Instead of the workclothes I used to wear at the warehouse I now wore a suit and tie—I was a white-collar worker! It suddenly dawned on me that I was being rewarded for having worked so hard at the warehouse, although my motive was simply to hold on to my job: advancement seemed too remote to think about.

The first thing I noticed about the mailroom, where all

kinds of office supplies were kept, was that it was a total mess. Secretaries used to walk in for stationery, pencils, steno books, etc., and they left the shelves in a lot less than apple-pie order. The head of the mailroom seemed so busy organizing the pickups of all the office correspondence that had to be mailed and delivered that he ignored the disarray of the shelves. Besides, he had to get by with an untrained replacement—me—instead of his regular assistant, so he thought he didn't have time to worry about cosmetics. This turned out to be my good fortune.

That first day on the mailroom job I stayed five or six hours after everyone had left and I rearranged all the shelves. Everything was neatly organized when I left the office at around midnight. Compared to the kind of physical labor I had been doing in the shipping room, this was really a breeze, although it didn't look that way to the people who came into the mailroom the next day. The effect was dramatic.

All I had anticipated was a simple thank-you from my temporary boss, but I was overwhelmed by what actually happened. When word spread throughout the office about what I had done, everyone came in to take a look and congratulate me on a fine job. The result was that I was not sent back to the shipping room but was given a chance to work in the bookkeeping department as a beginner.

Some years later I became office manager of the company and in addition to hiring and firing the mailroom personnel, I used to recommend the advancement of those I thought outstanding. By outstanding I mean this: making sure that there was enough soap and paper towels in the bathroom; filling the executives' water pitchers on time—all sorts of menial chores of that kind. Those who performed those functions perfectly were recognized by me for jobs in the editorial, advertising, sales, etc. departments—as beginners, to be sure—and all because *they did their best at the job they were supposed to do.*

I remember one young office boy whom I had to reprimand for having forgotten to fill Max Schuster's water pitcher one morning. His reaction was to argue that his college major was English literature, not filling water pitchers, and that the sooner he got out of the mailroom, the better. However, when an opportunity arose for me to recommend someone for advancement as an assistant to an editor, I chose a person who had demonstrated the ability to meet whatever menial responsibilities were involved in the job at hand—*without regard to that person's literary qualifications*! And I was proven right numerous times in using that approach. Namely, the person who fulfills the responsibilities of the job at hand is most likely to do so at the next higher level, no matter what the subject area might be.

Other dramatic examples bearing proof of this thesis come to mind. For instance, I recall the time that Letty Cottin Pogrebin came to work for Simon and Schuster as an assistant to Mildred Marmur, who was then my assistant in the subsidiary-rights department. When Letty came to work for us, her tasks were inordinately menial: filing, answering the phone, running errands, etc. However, she did whatever was asked of her so well that she soon was asked to take on more and more responsibilities. After only about six weeks, during which time I had been on a trip to Europe, I returned to find that Letty was practically ready to take over my job. I mean that seriously. She had actually done her best to learn everything she possibly could about our department and you would have thought she had had a decade of experience in subsidiary rights.

Soon after she left us, Letty Cottin Pogrebin became director of publicity, advertising, and subsidiary rights for Bernard Geis. When she was still in her early twenties she planned the promotion campaigns of many best sellers, including *Valley of the Dolls* by Jacqueline Susann and *Sex and the Single Girl* by Helen Gurley Brown. The pro-

49

motion of those two books launched their authors on the road to their highly successful careers and Helen Gurley Brown said, "I think Letty invented book promotion."

Some years later Letty wrote a best seller of her own entitled *How to Make It in a Man's World*. I would like to quote from it in connection with the theme of this chapter: controlling your life by doing your best. Here is what Letty wrote:

"If you start thinking about it early enough, you can mastermind your own progress to a remarkable degree. Norman Vincent Pealish as it may sound, you *can* control your own destiny. What is required of you, I think, is a realistic appraisal of your talents and a steadfast attention to your goals. In other words, what can you do best, where do you want to do it and how much time will it take you to get there?"

A few pages later, under a heading entitled "Be Incredibly Curious," Letty wrote:

"While doing her time . . . a girl should be reacting like a seismograph to everything around her. What information is on those royalty statements you've been typing since the tenth of the month? Is the composer making more money from records or sheet music? What percentage of the retail price of a book does the author receive—and where does the rest go? How did the mail-order advertising layout that you delivered to the client last month pull in the way of cash orders? Who founded the company and how long ago? What does a profit-and-loss sheet look like? What's a self-liquidating premium? Which is your company's main selling season? Most successful product? Most lucrative territory?

"As a secretary you can sponge up all the spilled information that no one even realizes is trickling in your direction. Instead of merely typing, you can test your new-found knowledge as you go. Read the incoming mail attentively. Be sure you understand everything referred to in an outgoing letter. Ask yourself questions about forms. *Read* contracts as you fill in the provisions. Ask your boss to explain technical terms. You're not being an under-cover Judas. You really will serve him better (though for a shorter time) if you grasp the meaning behind all your tasks, however menial."

Think about that final sentence: "You really will serve him better (though for a shorter time) if you grasp the meaning behind all your tasks, however menial." I like the parenthetical "for a shorter time," which brings us back to the boy who wanted to be promoted out of the mailroom but considered filling water pitchers too menial. As a result, he filled them for a much longer time than he really had to.

Only when you are doing your best, at whatever you are doing, are you controlling your life—assuming that your aim is to succeed. (Besides being subject to the will to live, we are also subject to the will to fail, as Dorothea Brande explains in *Wake Up and Live!**) Controlling your life requires you to repress negative impulses and express those that are positive, even if they relate to low-level or menial undertakings. Otherwise, failure soon becomes a bad habit.

In *The Descent of Man,* Charles Darwin wrote: "The highest possible stage in moral culture is when we recognize that we ought to control our thoughts." In other words, we must not merely learn to control our actions, but our thoughts as well. For me that's a lot easier said than done. My thoughts often run wild, although I can keep them from determining my actions. (Otherwise I'd be in jail.) However, by turning my thoughts into wishes whenever possible, I find that I have improved my ability to control them. For example, I used to think of ways to

*See page 82.

51

pad my expense account in order to supplement my income. Then I read *The Magic of Thinking Big* in which David Schwartz stated that cheating your employer was a prime example of thinking small. If instead you directed your thoughts into wishing you could be more productive for the company, you would be likely to come up with ideas that would lead to a raise. Instead of making *arithmetical* progress (by padding your expenses), you would be making *geometrical* progress (by getting a raise and improving your business position).

The jails are filled with crooks who worked very hard to be incarcerated. If they had spent half that time and energy in legitimate pursuits, think how far they might have gone. Most of us, in less harmful ways to society, spend a lot of time and energy in defeating ourselves. Once we take the first step of becoming aware that we are doing this, we are on the road to recovery. That awareness is a potent serum that wipes out the virus of failure.

As an exercise, think of the last five significant things you did and then evaluate how well you did them in terms of your ability. Were they up to your best? If not, why?

Do this exercise every day for a week and you will be amazed at the change that will take place. For one thing, you will begin either to do your best at a particular endeavor or you will decide not to do it at all. At that point you will have begun to take full charge of your life. You will have raised your consciousness as to what you are doing, why you are doing it, and above all, *how* you are doing it. As the saying goes, "It's not *what* you do but the *way* that you do it!" And that is the secret of how to control your life—and get what you want.

6

MENTAL JUDO: PUTTING THE INTELLECTUAL STRENGTH OF OTHERS TO YOUR OWN USE

Judo is a physical contest in which knowledge of anatomy and the principle of leverage are combined so that the strength and weight of an adversary are used to your advantage. The judo principle can also be applied *mentally* if you substitute the words "psychology" for "anatomy" and "learning and experience" for "strength and weight." Mental Judo, which I will call MJ, could then be defined as an intellectual confrontation in which your knowledge of psychology and the principle of leverage are combined so that the learning and experience of another are used to your advantage.

Almost all negotiating situations involve MJ to some extent, and it is an invaluable tool in accelerating the fulfillment of wishes. First I will give an example of how I used MJ in getting a raise in salary some years ago. At that time my boss felt that I deserved a raise but did not believe he could get approval from the chief financial officer of the firm because of the depressed economic climate.

He suggested that I make an appointment to see the chief financial officer and plead my case directly.

When I walked into the chief's office, quite apprehensively, he put me at my ease immediately by suggesting that we sit around the coffee table at one end of his large office rather than use the more formal chairs around his desk. He was actually using MJ on me right then and there by establishing a friendly, personal atmosphere in which he could make a denial of my request appear to be a kindly gesture rather than an outright rejection. Also, in a relaxed atmosphere I was likely to be much more candid about what I was actually doing on the job as opposed to exaggerating my accomplishments. The result was that when he did turn down my request, he made it seem as though he did so with my best interests at heart.

Feeling somewhat discouraged, but not wanting to give up, I decided to use some Mental Judo of my own. I asked the executive what *he* would have said had our positions been reversed. In other words, what arguments would he have used, what responses would he have given, if he were asking *me* for a raise.

The result was amazing. He reacted as though he couldn't wait to be the great teacher and gave me the best advice I had ever received on how to get a raise. He went so far as to have me explain my job to the last detail so that he could suggest the specific things I might have said that would have justified his giving me a raise.

Well, when he had finished giving me the benefit of his expert advice, I half-smilingly said that I was going to ask his secretary for another appointment with him, now that I knew what to do and say. At that he broke into a smile and said I could save time for both of us: he would give me the raise now!

That illustrates the use of Mental Judo in that I had used a chief executive's superior knowledge to get him to do what he hadn't intended—to change his mind—and there is nothing immoral or harmful or unethical about it. If I had not actually been entitled to a raise, I would not have gotten one despite the use of Mental Judo. That stratagem works only if it can be backed up by performance. For example, an understudy may become a star overnight because someone breaks a leg; but the understudy had better have the necessary talent to begin with.

The most effective way to use Mental Judo is to be absolutely honest about your inferior knowledge of a given subject, and then to ask for help. How many experts have refused to give you the benefit of their advice when you have asked for it? Haven't they often seemed delighted to be helpful?

When I started publishing books I knew little about the production end of the business. Most of my experience had been in the editorial and marketing and promotion areas. Fortunately, I met Walter Simson, the president of Rolls Offset, a company that manufactured all kinds of printed matter, including books. At the outset I told Walter that he could charge me whatever price he thought was fair—there was no use expecting me to evaluate the costs because I didn't know the first thing about them. The upshot was that I did business with Rolls Offset for twenty years that went into the millions of dollars. If Walter had cheated me out of only 10 percent of the total, it would have amounted to hundreds of thousands of dollars; but I would have been out of business, and Rolls Offset would not have done as well.

The point is that when I admitted my lack of knowledge of book production to Walter Simson, he was encouraged to try to teach me the basics at first, and then the fine points. But if I had been less candid I would not only have missed an educational experience, but would undoubtedly have been charged more for the manufacturing services I had received.

In his autobiography, Benjamin Franklin gives a number of examples of his use of Mental Judo, although he does not call it that. One application of Mental Judo by Benjamin Franklin comes to mind and I will let the master tell it in his own words. After stating that he was running for reelection as clerk of the General Assembly in Philadelphia, he writes:

". . . A new member made a long speech against me, in order to favor some other candidate. I was, however, chosen, which was the more agreeable to me as, besides the pay for the immediate service as clerk, the place gave me a better opportunity of keeping up an interest among the members, which secur'd to me the business of printing the votes, laws, paper money, and other occasional jobs for the public, that, on the whole, were very profitable.

"I therefore did not like the opposition of this new member, who was a gentleman of fortune and education, with talents that were likely to give him, in time, great influence in the House, which, indeed, afterwards happened. I did not, however, aim at gaining his favor by paying any servile respect to him, but, after some time, took this other method. Having heard that he had in his library a certain very scarce and curious book, I wrote a note to him, expressing my desire of perusing that book, and requesting he would do me the favor of lending it to me for a few days. He sent it immediately, and I return'd it in about a week with another note, expressing strongly my sense of the favor. When we next met in the House, he spoke to me (which he had never done before), and with great civility; and he ever after manifested a readiness to serve me on all occasions, so that we became great friends, and our friendship continued to his death. This is another instance of the truth of an old maxim I had learned, which says, 'He that has once done you a kindness will be more ready to do you another, than he whom you yourself have obliged.' And it shows how much more profitable it is prudently to remove, than to resent, return, and continue inimical proceedings.''

Rather than try to ingratiate himself to the influential gentleman, Franklin applied the judo principle and asked for a favor instead. This principle of reverse psychology, which I call Mental Judo, is to the process of knowing what you want and getting it what nuclear power is to a spaceship: it is a kind of fuel that moves serious wishing from the abstract to the tangible, i.e., from conception to consummation. I will explain this further, but first would like to clear up what might seem to be a negative aspect to the phrase Mental Judo.

On the surface Mental Judo may seem to be a tool for *manipulation*, a word with pejorative connotations. However, there are two kinds of manipulation: constructive as well as destructive, and we are always having to use the former in our human relationships. Parents manipulate their children as much or more than male chauvinists manipulate the women in their lives. The first is ethical but the second is not. The ethics are often determined by the ends that are served, not by the means that are used. If you hit a drowning person on the chin in order to save his life, would you not consider that act of violence justified?

Mental Judo in itself is not a bad thing. It is simply a process that can be used to produce desired results. It is actually an important technique in the art of negotiation, and I call it Mental Judo not only because it accurately describes the process, but also seems to be a catchy phrase that will help dramatize its existence. Perhaps someday there will be analyses of the different categories of Mental Judo such as Business Judo, Social Judo, Legal Judo, etc. In the meantime, it is my purpose to emphasize the availability of this important tool and to show how it relates to getting what you want.

Once you know what you want, know what your wishes are in every detail, the main body of your thinking will be constructively wish oriented. This means that you will constantly be reaching out—subconsciously most of the time—for the things you want that are beyond your grasp. Having raised your consciousness with respect to the use of Mental Judo you will now avail yourself of it at every opportunity. It was there all the time, but if you weren't aware of it, you undoubtedly let opportunities for its use pass you by. Instead of letting someone persuade you to do something you really don't want to do, or influence you to accept a situation that you are not happy with, you will now be listening with a different pair of ears.

For example, I had always wished to write songs with Sammy Cahn, one of the greatest lyricists of our time. His string of hits could fill a book (they actually do!) and they include such songs as "All the Way," "Love and Marriage," "Time After Time," "Three Coins in the Fountain," "Be My Love," etc. When I first met him some years ago, I automatically thought that he would never write with me, an unknown writer. Of course I turned out to be right. A negative attitude guarantees a negative result. Some years later I had the opportunity to meet Sammy Cahn again, only this time I applied a little MJ to my wishing and things turned out differently. You see, I had heard Sammy say that when he hears a musical theme it immediately suggests words to him and he can't resist the urge to write to it. Instead of asking Sammy to consider writing with me, I simply sat down at the piano (we were at a party) and played one of my original themes. In a few moments Sammy came over to me and asked what I was playing. No sooner did I tell him that it was an original melody than he wrote a lyric for it right then and there. (Incidentally, he is the fastest writer I have ever met. Some of his biggest hits were written in about the time it took him to type the words. Incredible but true.)

I am happy to say Sammy Cahn and I are still writing together and all because I not only dared to wish for that to happen, but took positive action: instead of asking him to write with me I applied a little MJ to get *him* to start the ball rolling.

This example emphasizes further that the use of MJ is not a selfish act. On the contrary, its successful use means that you have to look at things from the other person's point of view. You must always know what motivates the other person, and that necessitates a certain amount of compassion, understanding, and empathy on your part.

The art of negotiating is to know what the other person wants and then to give it to him or her consistent with your own interests. MJ simply accelerates the consummation of a negotiation but does not change the issues and aims involved. For example, suppose you wanted a friend of yours to go to a certain meeting with you. You know beforehand that your friend will be reluctant to go, so there is no point in simply asking him or her to go with you. However, you also know other things about your friend, perhaps one or more of these: he or she

1. would like to meet a certain person of your acquaintance;
2. delights in having dinner at a Japanese restaurant;
3. loves to play tennis at every opportunity;
4. wants to see a certain play or hear a certain opera.

Obviously you might now use any of the above factors as an incentive for your friend to attend the meeting with you. Instead of an empty plea—Please come with me!—you now use MJ. You say, "I've invited Bob Smith to come to the meeting. Since you've always wanted to meet him, why not come along too?" Or if (2) above is applicable, you might say, "After the meeting I'd like to take you to Seiko's for the Thursday-night special."

The more you know about other people, the subtler the forms of inducement can be. The subtler the inducement, the less likely is it to appear a quid pro quo, or worse, a bribe that will be resented. In order to win friends and influence people, you must know how to use people. In my opinion, there is nothing wrong about using people when it is to your mutual benefit. When you hear it said that it is wrong to use people, I think what is actually meant is that it is wrong to misuse people. So much for this lengthy apologia for Mental Judo lest it sound as though I'm protesting too much. The remaining question is how the MJ process ties in with knowing and getting what you want.

As I indicated before, MJ accelerates the transition of innermost desire from conception to consummation, from the wish to its fulfillment. In some cases it may be indispensable in achieving the desired result. When Harry Truman's vice president, Alben Barkley, was seeking the

Democratic presidential nomination in 1952 he needed the support of the labor leaders. President Truman advised Barkley to have individual meetings with each of the labor leaders during which he could get their promise of support. According to Truman, the leaders would be less likely to withhold their support if they met face to face *alone* with Barkley than if they all met together in a group. However, Barkley did not take the advice, and when he met the leaders in a group, one of them raised the negative factor of Barkley's age. At this, they all agreed that it was a major issue and their confrontation *as a group* was too much for Barkley to handle. Had he met them individually beforehand, Truman believed he could have mitigated the issue and gotten their promise of support.

Obviously President Truman was suggesting the use of MJ whether he called it that or not. Anytime you can control the collective mind-set of a group by first dealing with its individuals, you are putting the judo principle into practice. In businesses where decisions are made by boards of directors, this group technique is often used. Most of the executives who have climbed to the top have pretty much gotten support for their positions *before* rather than during or after the meetings. They have learned to sidestep *collective* bargaining. This is a principle to remember in any situation where you are dealing with more than one person: the principle of *individual* bargaining.

Think of how many of your wishes depend on your ability to persuade another person to do something. Not only getting a raise from your boss, but getting recognition in general depends upon your influence over others. That is why MJ is invaluable in accelerating wish fulfillment.

Many great performing artists—pianists, singers, etc.—have failed to gain recognition because they were lacking in showmanship. Similarly, many people of great potential have not achieved the acclaim or the appreciation one might have expected because they just used their own heads rather than the heads of others as well. It is not enough to use your head in solving life's many problems. You must also think of other people's heads as being available as well, and you will be surprised to see how often you will be able to put *their* minds to your own good use. That is the essence of Mental Judo.

Finally, bear in mind that judo is an activity in which no one is supposed to get hurt. True, as in any other contest such as chess or bridge, there are winners and losers. However, if a friend invites you for an enjoyable afternoon of chess, would you not consider the experience a plus whether you win, lose, or draw? In the same way, there are no losers when MJ is properly applied—only winners.

7

CREATIVE THINKING AND THE CROSS-APPLICATION OF PRINCIPLES

Earlier I discussed the fact that important principles of behavior can be revealed to us in cookbooks as well as in books on psychology. I also said that the principles involved in hitting a golf ball can be applied to selling real estate, or the lessons we learn from a study of counterpoint in music can be used in running a business. It is now time to elaborate on this concept.

As I mentioned earlier, some years ago I read the fascinating book by John van Druten, *Playwright at Work*. It is so filled with wisdom that I find myself rereading it from time to time. Although it deals specifically with the art of playwriting, I have applied its instructions to many other of my activities. For example, in the chapter about how to give *character* to the people in a play, John van Druten supposes that you want your hero to be a typical businessman. He writes: "Do you know the typical businessman? You know what he looks like, what he wears, but these things are not the man. Do not stick to the essentials. Do your best to avoid them, give him thoughts that you think the typical businessman might *not* have, interests that he might *not* have. Make him further and further from the apparently typical man in the insurance advertisements, and he will emerge exactly as you want him, and all the businessmen you meet will come and tell you how extraordinarily well you have drawn them." In other words, if you try to draw Mr. Average, you will end up drawing a blank, a dummy, and nobody will identify with him.

Having read that piece of advice from Van Druten, it struck me that he was espousing a universal principle, one that could have applications other than creating characters in a play. And I was right! Shortly after reading that I was called upon to write an ad for a book. At first I tried to write an ad that would appeal to everyone, men, women, doctors, lawyers, etc., and I was unsuccessful. Taking a lesson from John van Druten, I then tried imagining a real person I knew, one with many individual traits, likes and dislikes, and idiosyncrasies. I then wrote an ad that I mentally addressed to that *specific,* real person. As a result, I wound up writing an ad that had extremely wide appeal, whereas my first effort, which tried to reach everyone, reached no one.

Had I read *Playwright at Work* with the narrow idea that I would simply be learning how to write plays, I might have missed the foregoing "advertising" principle. However, I had long since learned to be alert to the possibility of applying what I learned from one subject to another.

Now I read everything as though it applies to everything, and as a result I pick up pointers about different things from the most unlikely sources. When I was telling a dear friend, Barbara Hubshman, about this recently, she told me that she did the same thing, and then surprised me with something I hadn't thought about: the philosophical meanings that you can find in simple nursery rhymes. For example, Barbara recited the familiar one about the cat that visited the queen:

> *Pussycat, pussycat*
> *Where have you been?*
> *I've been to London*
> *To look at the queen.*
> *And Pussycat, pussycat*
> *What did you there?*
> *I frightened a little mouse*
> *under her chair.*

Now, I had always thought of that bit of Mother Goose as nothing more than humorous nonsense until Barbara asked me to think about what it really meant. No sooner had she said that than I realized that I had made the same mistake again—I had overlooked the possibility of a nursery rhyme conveying a message. In this case the message is obvious once you realize that one is there: a cat will be a cat wherever she goes, even when she visits a queen. Or, in broader terms, what we really are as people will somehow manifest itself no matter where we go or what we do. And, even more important, when we are asked to tell about where we've been and what we have done, we will focus on what concerned us to the exclusion, perhaps, of the reality of the situation.

So what? If that's the message, couldn't we all have survived without receiving it?

Of course, but that's not the point. The point is that there are many, many messages of importance, principles of behavior, lessons in psychology, philosophy, etc., that we can easily miss if we are not alert to the *probability* of their presence. I say *probability* rather than *possibility* because you will miss less by using the former, rather than the latter, as your rule of thumb.

After the pussycat rhyme, Barbara recited the one about Humpty Dumpty. You know,

> *Humpty Dumpty sat on a wall,*
> *Humpty Dumpty had a great fall.*
> *And all the king's horses,*
> *And all the king's men,*
> *Couldn't put Humpty together again.*

Before Barbara got to the last line, I thought about my wife who had died of cancer about ten years before. At that time my friend Mike Shimkin, who knew she was dying, told me that if there was anything money could do to save her, I should not hesitate to ask him for it if we needed it. Unfortunately, it was one of those situations in life where all the king's horses, men, money—you name it—couldn't do a thing.

69

One of these days, thanks to Barbara, I will go back to Mother Goose and *A Child's Garden of Verses* and read them from a different viewpoint—the viewpoint that I have already been practicing with respect to other subjects. And this brings us back to John van Druten.

In *Playwright at Work*, Van Druten questions how many people you should tell about the play you are currently writing. He writes: "My answer is, as few people as possible. For me, there must be always one person around that I can talk to, discuss the idea with, and read scenes to as I write them. I need that person as I need a sounding board. I find it very hard to work entirely alone, though I have done so a couple of times. But more than one person is dangerous. Katherine Mansfield used to say that if she told the plot of any of her stories before she had written it, the story felt betrayed and frequently refused, thereafter, to be written at all. That is another of those slightly affected remarks, but I know exactly what she meant. I think the truer explanation is that if she had had the fun of telling the story, all that was left for her was work. The excitement, the sense of 'I've got a secret,' had gone in the telling, and work without fun is a dreary and unproductive business. There is fun in writing, and a great deal of the fun is the sense of having a surprise up one's sleeve."

I quoted John van Druten at length because I consider those words to be pearls of wisdom. They can be applied to any number of situations that most of us face in life even though we may not be playwrights. Earlier in this book I spoke of my invention of the game Bali and that most of my friends tried to discourage me from pursuing the idea. If I had read Van Druten's book at that time, I would have kept my mouth shut except for the "few people as possible" as he stated. There actually was a danger that I might have been affected by all the negative responses I received. Fortunately, I had already read Albert Carr's *How to Attract Good Luck* which insulated me to some extent from the negative fallout, but today I am armed in a twofold way. The first stems from Albert Carr's caveat, and the second from Van Druten's. This combination of restraints has led me to do many things I otherwise would only have talked about, and I urge you to reflect on that with respect to your own experience. Bear in mind, however, that there should be *one* person in your life who can be your sounding board for all kinds of matters—personal or business—that you may be considering.

In the introduction to a book about humor by Max Eastman, *The Enjoyment of Laughter,* I came across this passage:

"The mind should approach a body of knowledge as the eyes approach an object, seeing it in gross outline first, and then by gradual steps, without losing the outline, discovering the details. A book on American history, for instance—should begin by telling in a few sentences the author's conception of the significant form of that history as a whole. America was inhabited by Indians, Europe discovered it, certain phases of development were passed through, and we arrived at the Great Depression*—not more than a page. Then should follow a chapter giving the history of America from the Indians to the Depression, and laying in the fundamental explanatory factors, historical, racial, geographical, and economic. Then should follow three or four chapters giving the history of America from the Indians to the Depression, and elaborating these factors. Then should come six or eight chapters giving still further fundamental factors, but some glimpse also of the more subtle elements that developed between the Indians and the Depression. Then should follow eight

---

The Enjoyment of Laughter was written in the late 1930s when we had not gotten beyond the Great Depression.

71

or ten chapters in which race, economics and geography retire toward the fringe of consciousness, and the web of the story becomes visible—but still the full story from the Indians to the Depression. Then perhaps a book of twelve or fifteen chapters could be written, similar to those we now have, giving the history of America from the Indians to the Great Depression."

Now, Max Eastman's book was the least likely place (so it seemed) for me to learn something about the process of education. Nevertheless, that passage showed me not only how best to teach a subject but how to learn one as well. At present when I want to learn a new subject—abstract art, for example—I make it my business to get a good bird's-eye view of the *whole* subject before learning any of the details. Likewise, when I teach a subject—playing the piano by ear, for example—I explain what harmony and counterpoint are all about in no more than fifteen or twenty minutes. Then when I explain what a C chord is, or an F or a G chord, my student understands its relationship to all the other chords and knows how and when to use it when playing the familiar popular songs. Had I read Max Eastman's book from the point of view of humor alone, I would have missed a very important principle that I was able to apply many, many times.

Another book that taught me a great lesson in personal relations was *Between Parent and Child* by Dr. Haim Ginott. Although the book was concerned solely with child-parent relationships, I did not read it as though it were restricted within those boundaries. Instead, I allowed myself to consider Haim Ginott's advice from the point of view of behavior between adults as well as between adults and their children. I say "allowed" because we often must consciously extend the boundaries of our thinking in order to benefit from principles that have many possible applications.

In this book by Dr. Ginott I read that "statements of

understanding should precede statements of advice or instruction" when dealing with children in certain situations. He gives the example of a boy who looked forward to a picnic that had to be canceled because of rain. That was no time, according to Dr. Ginott, for his mother simply to tell the boy to forget about it and find something else to do. That would only antagonize the already disappointed child and make him feel misunderstood. The better thing to do would be for the mother to acknowledge the boy's feelings of frustration. She might say something like, "I can imagine how disappointed you must be." In that case, the boy's feelings would be assuaged by his mother's expression of sympathy, and he himself might venture a shrug of the shoulder and an, "Oh, well, I guess I'd better find something else to do," as Dr. Ginott says actually happened in that example.

Shortly after I read that passage, my wife was bringing food to the table and accidentally dropped one of the dishes. That was no time for me to say what was on the tip of my tongue: "Why did you have to carry so many dishes at the same time?" Instead of the "statement of advice," I took Dr. Ginott's advice and offered a statement of understanding: "It's only a dish, and besides, I think it was slightly cracked before you dropped it." That wasn't the last time I used Dr. Ginot's precepts about dealing with children in my dealings with adults.

It doesn't take much creative thinking to apply what you learn from child psychology to adult psychology. After all, most of us are only grown-up children anyway. However, I know that if I hadn't read Dr. Ginott's book from the point of view of *adult* behavior, I would have missed a lot. That is why it is important to remind yourself from time to time not to imprison various principles in restricted boundaries. Let them be free to be applied to as many different sets of conditions as human endeavor makes possible.

From time to time I bring up the subject of rereading various books, reviewing notes that remind us of the past, and doing other things that help to remind us of what was going on in our minds then. The reason I urge this practice is that one of the essentials of creative thinking is to make periodic assessments of our past assumptions. In order to look at things in a new way, we must challenge our past assumptions. Otherwise we become trapped by outdated prejudices, misinformation, and beliefs. To illustrate what I mean, I include two problems from a great book, *Lateral Thinking*, by Edward de Bono. The first one involves nine dots as shown below. The problem is to link these dots using only four straight lines without lifting the pencil from the paper.

"At first it seems easy and various attempts are made to link up the dots. Then it is found that one always needs more than four. The problem seems impossible.

"The assumption here is that the straight lines must link up the dots and must not extend beyond the boundaries set by the outer line of dots. If one breaks through this assumption and does go beyond the boundary then the problem is easily solved as shown."

THE PUZZLE

. . .

. . .

. . .

THE ANSWER

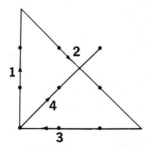

Here is the second problem:

"A man worked in a tall office building. Each morning he got in the lift on the ground floor, pressed the lift
button to the tenth floor, got out of the lift and walked up
to the fifteenth floor. At night he would get into the lift on
the fifteenth floor and get out again on the ground floor.
What was the man up to?

"Various explanations are offered. They include:

"The man wanted exercise.

"He wanted to talk to someone on the way up from
the tenth to the fifteenth floor.

"He wanted to admire the view as he walked up.

"He wanted people to think he worked on the tenth
floor (it might have been more prestigious) etc.

"In fact the man acted in this peculiar way because he
had no choice. He was a dwarf and could not reach higher
than the tenth-floor button.

"The natural assumption is that the man is perfectly
normal and it is his behaviour that is abnormal.

"One can generate other problems of this sort. One
can also collect examples of behaviour which seem
bizarre until one knows the real reason behind it. The

purpose of these problems is just to show that the acceptance of assumptions may make it difficult or impossible to solve a problem."

It is interesting to note that De Bono gives the following definition of a problem in *Lateral Thinking:* "A problem is simply the difference between what one has and what one wants." Here again is confirmation of how important it is to know what one wants.

In *The Art of Creative Thinking*, my good friend Gerard I. Nierenberg poses the following:

"You are asked to add a character to IX to make a six. If you have difficulties, think of how you are thinking of a six: as a Roman numeral, as an Arabic numeral, or as a word. If it is in the last system, the solution becomes obvious: SIX."

We must constantly challenge our long-held assumptions if we are to solve life's problems creatively, and as Edward de Bono expressed, solving our problems means we are fulfilling our wishes. Just as we must extend the boundaries of our thinking in order to solve the nine dots problem, we must extend them to make most of our wishes come true. By practicing the cross application of principles we are actually exercising the muscles we need to extend those boundries. If you keep this in mind, you will be surprised at how many opportunities you will have in your daily life to practice the cross application of principles, and therefore, to accelerate the process of getting what you want.

8

MAKE EVERYTHING THE BEST

I call this chapter "Make Everything the Best" instead of "Make the Best of Everything" because the latter implies settling for the status quo rather than trying to change things for the better. Change and rearrange, change and rearrange—that is the key to getting out of the rut and onto the road that leads to where you want to go.

Whenever you have time on your hands look around you and ask yourself what in your life can be changed or rearranged. Nine out of ten times whatever you decide to change or rearrange will result in an improvement. It stands to reason therefore that the more you change and rearrange, the more will you be improving things, and continuous improvement brings you closer and closer to the ideals you are seeking.

You have the power to turn liabilities into assets and bad luck into good. The first step is to realize that thousands of people have done just that, and they have done it by recognizing two important facts:

1. They began with an awareness that having bad luck and liabilities can be a blessing in disguise;
2. They realized that they themselves were the cause of many of the obstacles that blocked them from knowing what they wanted and getting it.

Let's examine the first of the statements: Successful people look upon the setbacks that occur from time to time as possible opportunities for the future rather than as permanent reverses. In other words, setbacks can be blessings in disguise. I can give you an example from my own experience.

After having worked for Simon and Schuster for eighteen years, from office boy to an officer of the firm, Max Schuster asked me to resign. In effect, he fired me. When he did, I thought it was the end of the world. As it turned out, I eventually formed my own company, which I would never have done had I not been pushed off the dock and forced to swim.

When Max Schuster requested my resignation, I immediately went to see Leon Shimkin, who at that time had become Schuster's partner in the ownership of Simon and Schuster. "I need your help. This is a crisis in my life," I said to Leon Shimkin. Hearing this, he told me to calm down and do some constructive thinking. He told me that the Chinese had no equivalent for the word *crisis*. They used the combination of the symbols for *danger* and *opportunity* to represent the meaning of the word *crisis*. "Therefore," said Mr. Shimkin, "take a lesson from the Chinese and realize the fact that while there may be some danger in your situation, there also may be some opportunity that should not be overlooked."

The result of Leon Shimkin's advice was that I reflected on what opportunities could possibly be available under the circumstances. After considering numerous possibilities, such as becoming a literary agent or book packager, I realized that if I could persuade my banker to finance me, I was now free to use all the contacts I had developed through the years with authors, publishers, and literary agents to form my own publishing company. That is exactly what I did, and I now thank God for what Max Schuster did, although it seemed like a fatal blow to my career at the time. Had he not forced my resignation, I probably would have remained in the same job for the next twenty years.

Whenever anything happens to me that seems to be bad luck at work, I always look for ways to benefit by the experience, and I almost always do.

The sports pages are filled with stories of great athletes who won Olympic medals because they tried to overcome some physical handicap they suffered when they were children. Likewise, the biographies of the greatest actors and comedians almost always refer to their shyness and the feelings of inferiority that they sought to overcome by playing a part and becoming somebody else. Demosthenes became a great orator because he tried desperately to overcome a speech defect he suffered in his youth.

Think of the worst things that happened to you in your life and reflect on whether you ultimately benefited from the experience. If you didn't, the chances are that you did not make it a point to discover the opportunities that were available as a result of your mishap. From now on, however, you will think twice before you allow any misfortune to throw you into despair; and more often than not you will find a way to capitalize on your "bad" luck.

For example, a publisher friend of mine lost a copy of *How to Sell Yourself to Others* by Elmer Wheeler. He became very upset when he found that he couldn't replace it because bookstores no longer carried it. But he viewed this as an opportunity and arranged to republish a new revised edition. It turned out to be one of his most profitable ventures.

Another example of this kind of thinking concerns a friend of mine who came to New York to close a deal for a syndicated cartoon strip that she created. When she arrived in New York, she learned that the cartoon-strip deal could not be closed because the syndicate had gone bankrupt. She was thoroughly chagrined over that bad news and didn't know what to do. However, being a determinded, positive-thinking person, she did not lose all hope. When she learned that a greeting-card fair was taking place for the benefit of greeting-card jobbers throughout the country, she rented a booth at the fair and transformed her cartoon characters into greeting-card characters with appropriate captions for all sorts of occasions. The result was that she took orders from the jobbers for thousands of greeting cards even before she had gone into production! Soon after that she became a young multimillionairess as the president of a lucrative greeting-card company.

Again, I want to emphasize the importance of looking upon any adversity as a potential stroke of good luck.

Once you begin to do this consciously, you will start to do it automatically, and for others close to you as well as yourself. The rewards will be enormous, not only in tangible terms, but you will find yourself emotionally stronger and better able to accept the reverses that are a part of life.

Incidentally, whenever you are feeling very sad or depressed, bear in mind the fact that your capacity for unhappiness reflects your capacity to experience an equivalent degree of happiness. Without the ability to feel great pain, you would not have the sensitivity to feel great joy. A cow in a pasture may be contented all day long, but just as sure as she cannot become grief-stricken, she cannot experience the thrill of hearing great music, appreciating great art, or hitting a great golf shot!

Therefore, if you raise your consciousness enough so that your capacity for feeling despair is an asset rather than a liability, you will find it easier to weather the storms of depression and make the transition from frustration to satisfaction, from pain to joy.

Now let us consider the second of the statements with respect to improving our fortunes: It is we ourselves who often create the obstacles to our success.

In *Wake Up and Live!* Dorothea Brande wrote that besides having a will to live, to survive, and to succeed, we also have within us a will to fail. Why? For one thing, failure has its rewards. If you settle for an easy life of mediocrity instead of achieving your full potential, according to Miss Brande, "You will never have to feel the rancor of those whom you necessarily surpassed in competition;* you will never have to stand the cut of adverse criticism. You will never have to become aware of the malice of those who envy any success, however trivial. You will never have to back your opinions by argument when you are tired and would rather rest for new effort.

*See page 22.

Or, far deeper and more vital pain, you will never see the discrepancy between the finished work you can do and the work as you had hoped to do it. There is always that discrepancy to keep the honest worker really humble.

"These matters of discomfort and pain evaded are important to notice, for when we come to examine the reasons why we so often choose to fail rather than to succeed, they will prove very illuminating. So it is worth understanding that *if you fail you are rewarded* by not running the risk of getting hot and tired and discouraged, or sharp-tempered when your co-workers or your materials, whatever they are, seem more refractory than usual. If someone else does excellently in the line you had dreamed of for yourself, you can always believe that, if you had really tried again, you could have surpassed him."

This theme of self-induced failure was discussed in *The New York Times* in an article by Bryce Nelson, "Self-Sabotage in Careers, a Common Trap." This article, published on Feb. 15, 1983, began as follows:

"The conflict is this: A powerful desire to achieve success is often thwarted by an even stronger fear of it.

"That debilitating fear of being successful, which some regarded in the 1970's as particularly prevalent among career-minded women, increasingly appears to be an abiding problem for members of both sexes. Indeed, at times, it seems to afflict almost everyone."

Further on, Mr. Nelson writes:

"What is common to people who fear success, psychiatrists say, is the conviction, rooted in subconscious conflict, that somehow success will bring with it some disastrous effect, such as isolation, punishment or abandonment. They may unconsciously dread being cut off or rejected by emotionally important people—parents, siblings, old friends or associates. And such fears can undermine, sometimes again and again, the efforts of bright and capable men and women to achieve, to accomplish what they want to accomplish.

"The fear, psychiatrists say, underlies the severe anxiety sometimes felt by people newly promoted. Such people, they say, may become sick or act in self-defeating ways that lead them to snatch a personal defeat from the jaws of their new victory."

What can we do, then, to conquer the negativism that seems to be inherent within us? How do we suppress the will to fail so that it does not control our lives?

The very first thing to do is to *be aware of its existence.* Once we realize that it is we ourselves—most of the time—who create the obstacles to success, we are then in a position to suppress destructive impulses in favor of those that are constructive; we are ready to eliminate the negative and accentuate the positive; we can begin the journey from failure to success.

Although some professional therapy may be advisable for those who suffer from intense fears over success, the prognosis should be good for the average person who simply becomes aware that he or she is the cause of the problem. Until I read *Wake Up and Live!* it never occurred to me that I had a will to fail within me. But when I started reflecting on that possibility, I began to realize how true it was. Equally important, I was able to free myself from subservience to the will to fail because I now had insight into the destructive games I was playing with myself. I had to laugh when I reflected on how I used to go out of my way to snatch defeat from the jaws of victory.

Then, if *being aware* is first, what is second?

According to Dorothea Brande, it is to "act as if it were impossible to fail." She arrived at that simple, yet profound, conclusion as a result of reading a sentence in F. W. H. Myers' *Human Personality* that changed her into a totally different person. I alluded to that sentence in the beginning of this book and it is now time to tell what it was. The most effective way to report it, and show how it led to Dorothea Brande's conclusion, is to quote her once again. She wrote:

"Consider for a moment the successes of a good hypnotist with a good subject: they sound utterly beyond nature, and for that very reason we have not learned from them all we might garner. . . . Perhaps one of the most remarkable cases is one cited by F. W. H. Myers in his chapter on hypnotism in *Human Personality*: a young actress, an understudy, called upon suddenly to replace the star of her company, was sick with apprehension and stage-fright. Under light hypnosis, she performed with competence and brilliance, and won great applause; but it was long before she was able to act her parts without the aid of the hypnotist, who stationed himself in her dressing-room.

"In the same chapter in which he quotes the remarkable case of the actress, Myers made a theorizing comment which is of immense value to everyone who hopes to free himself of his bondage to failure. He points out that the ordinary shyness and tentativeness with which we all approach novel action is entirely removed from the hypnotized subject, who consequently acts instead with precision and self-confidence.

"*Now the removal of shyness,* or mauvaise honte (he wrote), *which hypnotic suggestion can effect, is in fact a purgation of memory—inhibiting the recollection of previous failures, and setting free whatever group of aptitudes is for the moment required.*

"There is the clue. No sentence was ever more packed with rich implications for those who are in earnest about re-orienting their lives towards success."

She goes on to explain that we learn by "trial and error" and even though this leads to occasional success, does not cancel from our minds all the failures that went before it. "We succeeded at last, it is true; but meanwhile we experienced failure, sometimes ridicule, sometimes real pain, sometimes grave humiliation. We by no means retain in our memories only the item of the final success, nor does the success operate to make the failures and pain unimportant to our Unconscious.

"The Unconscious dreads pain, humiliation, fatigue; it bends its efforts even more ceaselessly to the end of avoiding pain than it does to the procuring of positive pleasures. So we are faced with a fact which at once accounts for much of the inactivity, the inertia, to which we succumb at moments when positive action would be to our advantage: *that rather than face the mere possibility of pain we will not act at all.*"

Accordingly, we allow our unconscious mind to protect us from the pain of possible failure and so we let our opportunities slip by for one rationalization or another. Thus we have allowed our *unconscious* to dominate our actions in our illogical attempt to avoid some possible discomfort. Therefore, says Miss Brande, "how convenient it would be if each of us could carry a hypnotist about, to cast his spell whenever we had to get to work! How marvelous if each of us could have his own private Svengali! Impossible, of course; and, more than that, undesirable. Fortunately, it is not at all necessary to be put under the sway of another's will in order to do our own work. The solution is far simpler. All that is necessary to break the spell of inertia and frustration is this:

"*Act as if it were impossible to fail.*

"That is the talisman, the formula, the command of right-about-face which turns us from failure towards success."

From the very moment that you believe in Dorothea Brande's analysis, and begin to act on her advice, you will begin to change your life dramatically for the better; you will be making everything the best.

To repeat what cannot be said too many times: *Act as if it were impossible to fail.*

9

WHY SOME PEOPLE I KNEW REACHED THE TOP

Many of the people I worked with during my years in publishing went on to become the chief executives of their organizations, and I was fortunate to be able to follow their careers and see how they managed the climb up the ladder of success. When I began to think deeply about this in connection with writing this book, I thought it would be a good idea to tell something about some of these people that would illustrate how they applied the principles that are the subject of this book.

I have always been a believer in reading about the experiences of successful people from all walks of life. While reading advance proofs of the autobiography of General Omar Bradley, I found it filled with examples of the principles of attracting good luck, the magic of believing, the power of positive thinking, the magic of wishing, and the power of knowing what you want. Despite the low interest I have in military affairs, General Bradley's story of his rise from obscurity and poverty to an esteemed place in history is a fascinating educational experience for me.

Each of the people I will profile certainly knew what he wanted—and got it. But their stories will also illustrate one or more of the other key principles that are the concern of this book. Therefore, you should read them as an exercise in discovering for yourself what particular principle is involved. Do this before you read my own short summaries at the end of each profile. (You might even find some principles that I missed.) In a few instances I named the principle involved, but for the most part I simply illustrated its application. A checklist of all the important principles begins on page 127. Just as all forms of exercise prepare you for the performance of certain functions, the exercise I now recommend will raise your consciousness and prepare you to recognize and use the particular principles that successful people use to achieve their goals.

After you have read the following brief profiles (which are presented in alphabetical order), I suggest that you think of some successful people you know and try to write a page or two about them. An easy way to start writing (particularly if you are not accustomed to it) is to make believe you are writing a letter to someone and want to describe the person in question; or simply make believe you're having a conversation about that person and just start talk-writing. (You would be surprised to know how many successful authors were encouraged by me to begin their books just that way.) At any rate, just reading the following pages should be beneficial; writing your *own* vignettes will reinforce the programming of your mind so that your wishes, like guided missiles, will automatically reach their targets.

A NOTE

During the course of my publishing career I had five bosses who were women, and they had my greatest respect and admiration. As far as I am concerned, each of them was fully capable of becoming the chief executive of the company although none did. You will look hard to find the name of a woman who is a president or chairman of the board of any major independent trade publishing company.

I believe it won't be long before this unfortunate situation is corrected, because I see more and more women heading various important departments, particularly advertising, publicity, and subsidiary rights. However, if I am to write about the heads of companies with whom I was involved, I am limited to men. (My son Robert accused me of male chauvinism when he read this manuscript, but I think my explanation relaxed him a little.) At any rate, the principles which are embodied in this book apply equally to either sex, and so I hope my women readers will be understanding.

Bill Adler

Bill Adler is president of Bill Adler Books, one of the foremost literary agencies and book packagers in the country. Phil Donahue, Dan Rather, Mike Wallace, President Reagan—these are some of Bill's clients.

Before Bill even met many of his clients for the first time, he began with a wish that they might write a certain kind of book. For example, while watching Willard Scott do his weather act one day on the *Today* show, Bill observed the joie de vivre that Scott seems to exude on every occasion. "Now there's a man who knows how to enjoy life," said Bill to himself, "and I wish he would write a book about himself and how he came to be that way." The result of Bill's wishing is *The Joy of Living* by Willard Scott, a wonderful book that is a story of self-fulfillment—a story of wishes that came true.

Bill Adler is good at a lot of things, but there is one at which he is by far the best in the business: he can come up with the right idea for the right book at the right time for the right author and the right publisher. On at least ten different occasions I have seen Bill do this within minutes after meeting a writer or a publisher while walking down the street or at a social gathering.

For about three years Bill and I used to walk home together every day—about a mile and a half walk from our offices—and from time to time we would meet someone he or I knew from the publishing world. One day we met Ralph Charell, an old friend of mine, and I introduced him to Bill. After a brief chat Bill and I walked on and I told him a little about Ralph. I said that he had been a stockbroker when we first met and later started to write books. One of his books included the best-selling *How I Turn Ordinary Complaints into Thousands of Dollars*, a book that caused Ralph to be listed in the *Guinness Book of World Records* as the world's most successful complainer!

"Ralph sounds like a man who *thinks rich*," said Bill, "and with his financial background, he certainly ought to know what he's talking about. Do you think he'd be interested in writing a book on the subject?"

"You certainly ought to ask him," I replied. Bill did.

Within one week Ralph signed a contract with Simon and Schuster to write a book entitled *The Magic of Thinking Rich*. The book turned out to be an excellent guide on the type of thinking or mental preparation that is essential if you want to achieve great wealth. In a sense, the book is about the process of wishing focused on the area of finance.

What we can learn from Bill is that we must not only think up ideas but we must try to execute them. We must not only know what we want, we must go out and get it. Not all of Bill's ideas turn out exactly the way they were envisioned, but a great many do—enough to make him one of the most successful people in the business.

I am sure you have heard a lot of people express new ideas that sound good, but how many of those people actually follow them up? How many even remember the ideas the next day, week, or month? Surprisingly few, I have found, and therein lies one of the most important lessons we can learn: don't just *think* while standing there; *do* something!

There is another essential ingredient of success and that is not to take no for an answer. That doesn't mean that we should beat our heads up against a stone wall, but too many of us accept negative reactions as though they were engraved in marble instead of trying to think up ways to achieve a positive result. Bill Adler once did something that epitomizes the way to react when a voice of authority says no. This is the kind of thinking all of us should try to do when faced with what appears to be a hopeless situation.

A few years ago Bill's mother-in-law was living in a relatively dangerous part of New York's Upper West Side. She was alone, had a bad hip injury, and to her chagrin found that her phone wasn't working. When a neighbor called the telephone company in her behalf, she was told that a repairman would come before 5:00 P.M. that day, which was a Friday. Unfortunately, no repairman showed up and Bill's mother-in-law was told that nothing could be done over the weekend; she would have to wait until Monday.

Well, you can imagine how frantic she was. An elderly lady with a health problem in a dangerous neighborhood would go out of her mind if she had to face a whole weekend without being able to communicate in an emergency. Her neighbor was planning to be away for the weekend and she would be left stranded. In desperation, she asked her neighbor to call Bill.

At this point, it was well after 5:00 P.M. and Bill knew it would be fruitless to try to get help through the normal channels. However, he realized that while it was after 5:00 P.M. in New York, it was only after 2:00 P.M. in California, so he called Pacific Bell and asked to speak to the vice-president in charge of public relations. (Bill knew that most people accept long-distance calls and so he more than half expected to be able to get the VP on the phone.) When the VP answered, Bill told him the story and said that surely, for reasons of national security, Pacific Bell had to be able to contact telephone repair people all over the country. Could they not contact New York and do something for his mother-in-law? The upshot: less than two hours later the phone was repaired!

I really love to tell that story because it proves how much one can do if the desire is there—the *wish*—and good, positive thinking is coupled with it. I admit that I am not nearly as ingenious a thinker as Bill Adler, either with respect to ideas for books, titles, or plain everyday problems. But even if I'm not as good, I'm still better off by making the attempt than by resigning myself to a status quo.

As I write these lines Bill is preparing to publish the *I Love America Diet* with Phyllis George as coauthor. (His *I Love New York Diet* with Bess Myerson was a national best seller.) Knowing Bill as I do, it would not surprise me to learn that he has started work on the *I Love Universe Diet*, with God as his coauthor!

The predominant principles of Bill Adler's successful behavior are numbers 3, 13 and 16 from the checklist (begins page 127). By welcoming the opportunity to meet new people, aiming directly for what he wants (specific book ideas for specific people), and thinking laterally (offices can be closed in New York when they're still open in California), he hits his target almost every time.

Robert L. Bernstein

Bob Bernstein is the chairman and chief executive officer of Random House-Knopf, one of the most prestigious jobs in publishing. I remember his first day in the business, some thirty-odd years ago, when he was being introduced to the employees of Simon and Schuster where he started as a lowly assistant in the sales department. At that time, I had a lowlier job as a clerk in the bookkeeping department, and I recall being somewhat envious and resentful of the attention Bob was getting as a new employee. Nobody ever took me around and introduced me when I came to the executive offices of S&S *after working my way up from the shipping room*.

Looking back, I can now easily understand and accept the difference in the way Bob and I were treated, not only on our first days but throughout our careers. The reasons were simple and quite apart from the fact that he had superior educational background, richer parents, and better business connections. This was true about most people in relation to me who joined the firm but I still managed to surpass them in terms of our careers. Not Bob, of course, who is not only well known in publishing circles, but renowned worldwide as one of this country's most articulate and effective spokesmen on human rights.

As I said, the reasons why Bob was treated differently from me—even on the very first day in his publishing career—were simple and boil down to three:

1. He knew what he wanted out of life. (I was confused about my aims and never really believed I would achieve them anyway.

2. He wasn't afraid to express his opinions even if it meant contradicting his superiors. (I used to tell my bosses what I thought they wanted to hear, not what I thought was the truth.)

3. He had confidence in himself. (I felt inferior.)

Let me give you a specific example that demonstrates the truth of the above three reasons.

About ten years after Bob came to S&S he had worked his way up to a high-salaried executive job in the sales department but did not feel that he was getting the recognition he deserved. In addition, Bob felt that he would do better working as an independent entrepreneur rather than as a corporate employee, so he left S&S and set up his own business enterprise. (There's an example of self-confidence for you.)

Shortly after Bob started his own business, Bennett Cerf, then president of Random House, asked Bob to join the sales department with the aim of eventually heading it. Bob resisted Bennett Cerf's solicitations until, as a last resort to get Bob, Mr. Cerf made the following unusual offer: he asked Bob to make a list of everything that would make him change his mind and come to Random House. Since Bob knew exactly what he wanted, he unhesitatingly wrote out his demands without regard to whether they would be agreeable or not. When Bennett looked at the list, he simply said "Bob—you've got it!"

At this point you might be thinking that if someone like Bennett Cerf made a similar offer to you, you would also know what to say. I submit the following questions:

1. Would you have known exactly what you wanted?*

*After having written the above about Bennett Cerf, I happened to meet Bob Bernstein at a cocktail party and told him about it. I said, "Bob, that story exemplifies the title of my book: you knew what you wanted and you got it." Bob, who is one of the wittiest people I know, immediately replied: "You mean Bennett knew what *he* wanted!"

2. Would you have tempered your demands in any way for fear of having them rejected?
3. Would you have had the confidence in yourself to give up a bird in the hand for a bird in the bush?

Try to answer the above three questions as honestly as you can because the better you are at self-analysis, the more likely are you to get what you want out of life. To this day I would have problems with each of the above questions, although not nearly as acutely as would have been the case twenty years ago.

According to some literary critics, the thrust of Marcel Proust's writings was to show us that the main thing we learn from experience is what kind of mistakes we will tend to go through life making over and over again. If that is indeed what Proust was trying to tell us I believe he was right. I see myself suffering from this malady as well as my friends. I am also reminded about a particular mistake of mine when I reflect on the differences between Bob Bernstein and me as I see them now and as I recall them twenty years ago. Specifically, where Bob was, and is, totally forthright (or brutally honest, as some might say), I still tend to tell people what I think they would like to hear—not because I want to mislead or deceive them, but because my ingrained feelings of inferiority impel me to try to win their affection and goodwill. Experience has made me aware that I am prone to make this mistake over and over again; and even though experience hasn't changed my personality or character, it has alerted me to keep that shortcoming within reasonable bounds. Although I said at the outset that a book can change your life, I did not say that it could change your character or personality. Despite our faults, and no matter how serious some of them may be, we can still succeed provided we are *aware* of them. That means we must see ourselves as others see us, but how do we do this? In my case, by comparing myself with Bob Bernstein early in our careers, I learned more about myself than about him. What I am suggesting, therefore, is that we make it a regular practice to compare ourselves with other people—particularly our peers—from time to time with respect to their talents, personal qualities, and behavior patterns. In the same way that teachers often learn as much or more than their pupils, the more we learn how others differ from us, the more we learn about ourselves.

Finally, about Bob Bernstein, more than anyone else I know he has the ability to choose the best person for a particular job and the self-assurance necessary to step back and allow that person to take charge. In other words, Bob knows how to delegate authority without losing a smidgen of his own. (There, by the way, is a prime example of how one gets more by giving more.)

The ability to choose the right people on whom to rely and then to feel secure enough to manifest that reliance is not only a key ingredient of success in business, but in our social lives as well. For some reason, there are people who can delegate authority in business but not in their personal affairs; there are others who have no problem with this *personally* but have to be involved with every minuscule business decision. An example of the latter is a working mother who can allow a housekeeper to make key decisions about raising her children, but becomes a tyrant in the office. Or, the executive who forces his wife to take total responsibility for rearing their children with no help from him, but insists on being consulted about every minute detail in the office.

Unfortunately, unless we can delegate successfully in both business and personal situations, we face a life of frustration and disappointment. To be able to delegate authority is the ability to accept advice, obviously a quality that is essential to success and happiness. I've given you the bad news. The good news is that we *can* develop and improve this ability by taking small first steps at the beginning and increasing them later. *Take advice and delegate authority* should be our motto, and one which we should put into practice at every opportunity.

Bob exemplifies the interaction of checklist principles 9, 10, and 17. He delegates authority with confidence (thus using other heads as well as his own), he knows what he wants, asks for it, and takes risks with confidence.

David A. Boehm

Dave Boehm founded the Sterling Publishing Company, publishers in America of *The Guinness Book of World Records*, among many other informational publications. The Sterling list has as many or more how-to books than any publisher I can think of. As a result, Dave himself is a mine of information on many different subjects.

The Guinness Book of World Records had its origin in England. The Guinness people, producers of the famous beverage, first issued it as a booklet to settle arguments in English pubs where their merchandise was sold. On one of his early trips to London, Dave Boehm came across the Guinness book and immediately recognized its potential. He acquired the American rights and today, besides publishing the book, is involved in exercising a variety of rights, such as radio, television, syndication, etc. There are even nine Guinness museums based on the theme of the book. The Guinness-book story therefore is a lesson in expanding the development of a property by thinking of it in more than one dimension. I have discussed this principle in chapter 7, particularly with reference to *The Art of Creative Thinking* by Gerard Nierenberg and *Lateral Thinking* by Edward de Bono. There is one other aspect to Dave Boehm's career that illustrates a basic principle indigenous to the art of knowing and getting what you want: the necessity to take calculated risks in changing jobs rather than playing it safe and staying in a comfortable rut.

Before he founded Sterling, Dave had experience in business, printing, editorial, sales, and book production. In order to get this variety of experience, he had to go from one company to another, often leaving a secure position to do so. Because he was willing to risk changing jobs, he became uniquely qualified to start his own publishing business, something he wished to do more than anything else.

In my own case with Simon and Schuster, I transferred from the bookkeeping department to the subsidiary-rights department. (In a book publishing company, the subsidiary-rights department handles the sales of such rights as motion picture, television, magazine, newspaper—any rights it can dream up, provided the author hasn't reserved them for himself.) I wanted to make this job change because it meant going from a service department to an income-producing department and that always leads to a higher salary. In bookkeeping the most I could do at the end of a year was show how diligently I worked—something I was supposed to do anyway. However, in selling rights, I had the opportunity to make some unusual—sometimes spectacular—income-producing sales, for which I stood a chance to get extra recognition and compensation.

I want to close with the story behind the name of Cornerstone Library and Dave Boehm's part in it because it is a fine example of the principle of thinking big as espoused by David J. Schwartz in his wonderful book *The Magic of Thinking Big*.

As I indicated earlier, Dave Boehm played a large part in the founding of Cornerstone Library, not only because he set up our structure for manufacturing our books, but because of his editorial and marketing suggestions, and even choice of the name. My close friend Michael Shimkin was trying to help me start the company, and he and I were trying desperately to come up with a good name. (Mike, by the way, is the son of Leon Shimkin, one of the most prominent publishing heads I will devote a section to later on.) At any rate, Mike and I had only about one day left to decide on a name that I could incorporate under and we wanted it to be right.

Since we were planning to publish basic, how-to instruction books, Mike first suggested the name Basic Books. However, I pointed out that Norman Rosenthal had already thought of that name for his own successful company. "How about Foundation Books or Publications?" asked Mike, to which I replied that the word "foundation" was usually associated with nonprofit enterprises and I was certainly hoping to go far in the opposite direction! However, Mike was on the right track so I suggested looking for synonyms of "foundation" in *Roget's Thesaurus*. Upon doing so we were struck by the word "cornerstone" ("keystone" sounded good, but had already been used). "Cornerstone Press," I shouted with great glee. "Let's call Dave Boehm and get his opinion."

Dave liked the word "cornerstone" very much, but he wasn't too happy with the word "press." "You could be a printing firm as opposed to a publisher." he said. "In view of the fact that you're planning to publish a collection of books on the same subjects—a whole library of books about chess, bridge, golf, tennis, etc., why not call yourself Cornerstone *Library*. Think big!" And the moment Mike and I heard those words, we knew that was it. That was the perfect name for the company.

In retrospect, Dave's suggestion seemed so obvious that we felt like fools for not having thought of it ourselves. However, that's true of some of the greatest ideas ever conceived by man. The cog in the wheel that causes its gears to make the jump from mediocrity to excellence is the process of thinking big, and that is what we must practice at every opportunity. The next time you are faced with any problem, and you arrive at what seems to be a satisfactory solution, pause for a moment and ask yourself, "Am I thinking big? What solution might I come up with if I broadened the scope of my thinking?" You will be surprised at the alternatives that will occur to you simply because you opened your mind wide enough to let them in. That is what Dave Boehm has been doing for most of his life, and if you have the good fortune to meet him, you'll know exactly what I've been trying to express.

Perhaps principles 11, 13, 17, and 18 are the ones that most often worked in combination with each other to bring about Dave Boehm's outstanding success. He grasped new subjects quickly because he viewed the forest before attempting to focus on the trees. The numerous job changes that he voluntarily made illustrate the confidence with which he took risks and rearranged his life.

Robert A. Gottlieb

Bob Gottlieb is the president and editor-in-chief of Alfred A. Knopf, now a subsidiary of Random House. I first met him about thirty years ago when he came to Simon and Schuster as an assistant in the editorial department. Jack Goodman was the chief editor in those days and Bob worked under him. Jack had a long list of prominent authors, including humorists such as James Thurber, S. J. Perelman, Walt Kelly, and Herblock, novelists like Meyer Levin, Romain Gary, and Rona Jaffe, as well as celebrities from Hollywood and Broadway like Steve Allen, Rocky Graziano, Jackie Gleason, Bing Crosby, and Bob Hope. Since Jack Goodman preferred partying with the famous rather than editing their works line by line, he turned over as much as he could to Bob Gottlieb, who benefited greatly from that exposure. When Jack Goodman died prematurely, Bob was already well qualified to make the contacts with authors and literary agents that resulted in his editing and sponsorship of such books as Joseph Heller's landmark *Catch-22* or Chaim Potok's *The Chosen*, or—but I could go on endlessly. You get the point.

What impressed me most about Bob was not his editorial capacity—I was not competent to judge that—but his excellent grasp of the business side of publishing. Many junior editors had the same opportunities for advancement that Bob had but none came close to his level of accomplishment. I believe that was primarily because Bob did not sneer at the commercial aspects of publishing, but made it his *business* to learn all he could about the *business*. At the very few advertising and promotion meetings I attended with Bob, he invariably came up with brilliant marketing suggestions one never ordinarily got from an editor. Also, in connection with the books he sponsored, he did not concern himself solely with editorial matters. He got involved in advertising, promotion, subsidiary rights, as well as how the books would be manufactured. In other words, he acted like a publisher rather than an editor well before he got the title. This is characteristic of most of those who reach the top: they assume much of the authority and responsibility of the job they are seeking well before they actually get it. This stems from their overpowering wish to get that job.

Some time ago I asked a dear friend of Bob Gottlieb if she knew what Bob was aiming for at the time he was still on the editorial staff of Simon and Schuster and there were several people between Bob's position and the top. Without hesitation she said that Bob's goal was to become the foremost publisher/editor of his generation—and that's exactly what he became. He *knew* what he wanted; he *got* what he wanted. It always follows, as I have pointed out before.

There is one more thing I'd like to say about Bob and it has to do with something that I was told by Strome Lamon. Who is Strome Lamon? In Bill Adler's recent book, *Inside Publishing*, you will find the following sentence on page 193: "Simon & Schuster has always done the best advertising in the business and that's because Strome Lamon is the best ad director in book publishing."

I purposely chose that quotation to identify Strome Lamon because it is significant in relation to what Strome said about Bob Gottlieb when I told Strome that I would be writing about Bob in this book. (For a short time Strome and Bob were colleagues at Simon and Schuster before Bob left to work for Knopf.)

In our discussion about Bob, Strome agreed with me that while Bob concerned himself primarily with literary matters, he never overlooked the commercial or financial aspects of any project. Then Strome said something that took me by surprise. He said that if he had to name one thing he learned about book advertising, it was something he learned from Bob; and when he heard Bob say it, it was as though he were listening to an Indian guru at the top of the highest mountain telling him a great universal truth such as "Life is a fountain!" What Bob said was that "a book ad should have lots of little things falling out of it."

According to Strome that statement of Bob's had more impact on him than all the books he had ever read about advertising. You can check the truth of that yourself the next time you look at a Simon and Schuster ad. You will notice immediately how many different interesting thought-provoking bits of information seem to hit you from all directions. You will have the feeling that if you could shake the page hard enough the floor would be filled with scraps of information about the book and/or author in question.

I asked Strome to elaborate on Bob's statement and tell me exactly how he put it into practice. Strome replied that Bob meant a book ad could be written as though you were bringing a major news event to the public's attention. In other words, just as you might see a screaming headline followed by sub-headlines about other aspects of an event when it is reported on the front pages, a book ad might boldly announce that AUTHOR SO-AND-SO HAS DONE IT AGAIN!—First Printing Sold Out Before Publication!! Fourth Printing now on Press! Soon to Be a Major Motion Picture—all this followed by quotes from what others are saying about the book. The ad, therefore, is not simply announcing that such-and-such book is being published, but it is breaking a major news story. History is being made!

I have gone into the above at length because it is a clear example of lateral thinking, or the cross application of a principle as discussed earlier in this book. Had Bob Gottlieb been a front-page newspaper editor before getting involved in book advertising, one might have expected him to arrive at his interesting approach. However, the disposition to see things in many different contexts rather than from narrow perspectives helps one to make significant judgments on the basis of vicarious experience. Bob clearly has that disposition. That is why he can run a big business without having taken a course in business administration. He was able to acquire the necessary expertise by extrapolating the principles he learned in other, unrelated fields.

Knowledge of counterpoint in music can help a doctor practice medicine; skill in hitting a golf ball can help you sell real estate. It should become second nature to you to grasp the principles pertaining to one field of endeavor and apply them in another. This is one of the secrets of getting what you want.

Bob's career is a perfect example of the way principles 13 and 19 work together. His comment about book advertising, for example, indicates a mind that functions three-dimensionally. The way he approaches his job as an editor shows how he exercised functions above and beyond the common boundaries of that position. Also, while it was usual in Bob's early days for editors and publishers to hold themselves aloof from the commercial aspects of the profession, Bob challenged those customary assumptions by paying as much attention to the business aspects of publishing as to the artistic.

Harold Roth

When I first met Harold Roth thirty-odd years ago, he had come to work for Pocket Books. Pocket Books then was not a subsidiary of Simon and Schuster but both firms were closely allied. Harold, though working in a relatively menial job for Pocket Books, came to the attention of the top executives of Simon and Schuster through his unique abilities.

One of Harold's unique abilities was his expertise at interviewing and evaluating potential employees for Pocket Books. His analyses and forecasts of personnel were so exceptional that he was consulted frequently by the executives of Simon and Schuster whenever they needed assistants. Within a relatively short time Harold rose from his menial job to one that ranked just below that of the two owners of the company.

However, Harold left his high-salaried, prestigious job at Pocket Books to work for Grosset and Dunlap. He left because he wanted to be the chief executive of a company, and that job wasn't in the near future at Pocket Books; no one succeeded Leon Shimkin to the presidency until about fifteen years later. Further, at what seemed to be against all odds (to everyone except Harold), he went on to become the president of Grosset and Dunlap. Harold knew what he wanted.

Before leaving Pocket Books, Harold Roth asked me to have lunch with him to discuss what I knew about Manuel Siwek, then president of Grosset and Dunlap. Manny Siwek had been a salesman for Horace Liveright, one of the most flamboyant book publishers who became a legend in his own time. Possibly through his association with Horace Liveright, Manny Siwek was encouraged to elevate himself culturally by collecting (and reading) a library of great books, and accumulating records of the greatest classical music.

The Siwek apartment, because of Manny, became a cultural oasis in a lower-middle-class, low-brow neighborhood in upper Manhattan. Manny's parents were proud of the way he was rising in the book-publishing field, and his salary of about seventy-five dollars a week was phenomenal in our neighborhood in those days. With Manny's encouragement, the entire Siwek family— parents, three daughters, two sons—seemed to be motivated by a desire to improve themselves intellectually and culturally, and to try to meet as many aspiring young artists and writers as they could.

In retrospect, I now realize how valuable it was for me to have been a neighbor of the Siweks and to have been exposed to their cultural interests. In the same way that exposure to certain people leads to good luck (as discussed in an earlier chapter), exposure to great works of art through museums, concerts, and libraries inevitably leads to successful wish fulfillment. For one thing, it helps us define our wishes and encourages us to make new ones; it provides essential input to our "human computer"—our brain—thereby programming us for a successful launch on the way to our target.

Manny Siwek also had a reputation for being a tough leader. Employees of his told me he was capable of firing an executive for showing up five minutes late to a meeting. When I told Harold Roth that he might find himself in a rough situation if he didn't hit it off with Manny, Harold couldn't have been more confident. Harold felt that he had proved his ability to survive the toughest challenges of "corporate politics" as a result of his rise at Pocket Books, and he was supremely confident of his chances at Grosset and Dunlap. The result, as I said before, was that in a short time he became president of the firm and Manny Siwek retired.

If you were to ask me what I believe to be the key attribute that led to Harold Roth's rise to the top, I would say it was his ability to learn what makes people tick. As I noted before, his in-depth evaluations of prospective employees were extremely accurate. That talent combined with positive thinking, doing the things that attract good luck, and knowing what he wanted out of life made it inevitable that his wishes would come true.

Harold Roth is an excellent example of a person who can use the principles expressed in numbers 15, 16, 17, and 20. I have tried to show how he was not afraid to change jobs when he believed his aim was off target. Also, he not only knew what he wanted, but acted with the confidence of one who felt he could not fail. In querying me about the company he was about to move to, he was not reluctant to admit that he could learn important things about the people from me.

M. Lincoln Schuster

Max Schuster and Dick Simon founded Simon and Schuster in 1924 and alternated each year as president and chairman of the board. I first met Max Schuster when it was my job to fill his pitcher with ice water every morning during the late 1940s. I was an office boy then, having graduated from the warehouse where I used to pack books. It was a thrill for me to be working in the executive offices, especially after the warehouse experience, and if Mr. Schuster or Mr. Simon said "Good morning" to me, it made my day. I never dreamed that someday I would be calling them by their first names and socializing with them. Although that was something I wished, I didn't see how it could ever happen—a negative attitude that delayed that wish coming true for at least five years.

Max Schuster always wanted to be a publisher and started working as an editor for The World, one of the best newspapers during the first quarter of this century. Dick Simon was a salesman for Horace Liveright, and so the two young men (in their early twenties) combined their editorial and sales experience to form Simon & Schuster, Inc.

Young Dick and Max did not have any immediate publishing plans when they opened their doors, and they were hard pressed to find publishable manuscripts. Luckily, Dick Simon had an aunt who came up with an original idea. She was a crossword-puzzle fan who couldn't find enough puzzles to satisfy her since they were only available in newspapers in those days. "Why not publish a book of crossword puzzles?" she asked. The two men responded favorably and the rest is history. Dick and Max thought though, that they might not be taken seriously as publishers by literary agents and authors if they started with a crossword-puzzle book. Therefore, they did not publish the book under the Simon and Schuster name, but used The Plaza Publishing Company as their imprint. Even years later when they could well afford to use the Simon and Schuster name, they continued for sentimental reasons to credit the publishing to The Plaza Publishing Company.

In an earlier chapter I said that the principles that apply to one activity can be applied with equal effectiveness to any other if you open your mind to that possibility. I actually learned that from Max Schuster, who asked me to sponsor a book along those lines. He suggested that whoever might be the author use the principles involved in the game of chess as the basis for a philosophy of life, illustrating the versatility and universality of sets of principles. Although I still haven't gotten around to acting on Max's suggestion, I may do so someday, unless someone else beats me to it.

Max Schuster used to read at least five or six newspapers a day, and he used to mark up articles for his secretary to cut out and file. He used different-colored crayons, each color denoting a different category. He also used to carry different-colored memo slips with him so that he could scribble down ideas wherever he happened to be. People in the office used to laugh at him (behind his back, of course) for doing this. However, they didn't laugh when they needed current information about any particular subject. On a moment's notice, Max's files could produce a book full of fascinating articles about almost any serious subject. These were of immense value to some of his authors like Will and Ariel Durant, the philosopher-historians.

When asked how long a book should be, Max used to say it should be like a woman's dress: long enough to cover the subject but short enough to be interesting. And if you asked him how he picked manuscripts, he would tell you that he picked editors: they picked manuscripts. Although he appeared to be reclusive, introspective, and aloof, he was a very warm and witty person who would offer whatever help he could give to anyone who dared to ask. I say "dared" advisedly because he didn't seem like the sort of person you could slap on the back and ask a favor of. However, just as Benjamin Franklin learned from the example I gave earlier, I learned that those who weren't put off by Max's exterior got whatever help they asked for from him. Unfortunately, I made the mistake of trying to do *him* a favor, and my solicitous attitude backfired. At the time I couldn't understand why this was happening, but I know better now, thanks to Benjamin Franklin.

One of Max Schuster's great contributions to the publishing industry was to show that there was a market for books about highly complex subjects if they could be written in everyday language. It began with *The Story of Philosophy* by Will Durant, a book that was disparaged by the critics, who thought it was too simplistic. Other publishing "experts" said the public would never buy it. After nearly sixty years it is still alive and selling well.

After *The Story of Philosophy* there were numerous "story" books about mathematics, music, chemistry—you name it. Even Albert Einstein* was persuaded to write *The Evolution of Physics* for Simon and Schuster, a book which the author tells the reader at the outset is "a simple chat between you and us." Imagine a simple chat with Einstein about physics! But Max Schuster wanted to bring the most sophisticated ideas as down to earth as possible for the sake of readers who he believed were thirsting for that kind of knowledge. He was certainly right and far ahead of his time. Today it wouldn't surprise me to find a book entitled *Brain Surgery for the Layman,* that's how far we have gone as a result of Max Schuster's pioneering efforts.

*In collaboration with Leopold Infeld.

Apart from the actual business of publishing, there is one incident involving Max Schuster that had an enormous impact on me. He asked me to contact a Broadway producer about my getting house seats to the producer's show so that I could see it and report to Max about it. After I did that and reported to him about the show, Max asked me to get seats for two other editors and their wives. I was reluctant to do this because I felt diffident about asking for further free seats to one of the hottest shows in town, and I didn't know the producer that well. When I told Max that I thought the producer might expect me to buy the extra seats, and that might be expensive, he became annoyed with me and said: "That's a detail and I don't like to be bothered with such details." In other words, he was admonishing me to think big and not let a matter of relatively small economics interfere with the objective.

The result was that I asked for, and got, the extra house seats. My earlier reluctance had been mitigated because I knew my expense account would have been approved had I had to buy the seats.

For some reason, the expression on Max Schuster's face and the sound of his voice when he uttered the words "That's a detail" have always lived with me. I am sure that I have brushed aside many objections that otherwise would have deterred me from doing something because of that long-held memory and the lesson I learned —think big!

As I indicated in this profile, I learned the very first principle from Max Schuster. Further, his constant recording of ideas that occurred to him was a reflection of principle 4. Other principles that seemed to have been operative were number 11 (which resulted in his publishing comprehensive yet simple books about complex subjects) and number 18. No man that I had met, including book reviewers, were better read than Max Schuster.

Leon Shimkin

Leon Shimkin started working for Simon and

Schuster about six months after the firm opened its doors. That was in 1924 when he was only seventeen years old and going to night school at New York University. Thirty-odd years later he became the owner of the company until he sold it to Gulf & Western Industries in 1975, and is now chairman-of-the-board emeritus.

One of Leon Shimkin's first accomplishments at the young firm actually enabled the company to stay in business when it was facing a possible major cash crisis. It came about this way: the successful publication of the crossword-puzzle book during the first year resulted in higher profits than had been anticipated. These profits were used to finance additional publications with the consequence that there wasn't enough money left over to meet the high tax bill the company suddenly faced.

Young Leon Shimkin came to the rescue. He persuaded the Internal Revenue Service to adopt a ruling that significantly lessened the tax burden of all book pulishers—not only Simon and Schuster—so that they could be in a better position to reinvest earnings for the benefit of their authors, the reading public, as well as themselves. It surprised no one when Leon Shimkin became the head of the business department shortly thereafter.

Although his primary responsibility was to manage the business affairs of the company, like all great achievers, Leon did not let his business title circumscribe his activities. He very soon involved himself in editorial matters with the result that he sponsored the publication of two of the most successful books in the history of publishing. They were the annual tax guide by J. K. Lasser, *Your Income Tax*, and Dale Carnegie's *How to Win Friends and Influence People*. The powerful drive that *wishing* gives to positive thinking is superbly illustrated by the story behind these two publications.

Leon Shimkin wanted to do everything he could to better himself as a business executive and when he heard about Dale Carnegie's course on public speaking he decided to take it. So impressed was he by the principles espoused by Mr. Carnegie that he asked him if he would consider writing a book on the subject. Mr. Carnegie said he was too busy to undertake such a project, but Leon Shimkin was not willing to take no for an answer. He suggested hiring someone to take notes at Dale Carnegie's lectures from which the material for a book could be organized and edited. The result was *How to Win Friends and Influence People.*

The story behind the Lasser tax book is a short one. Very simply, the idea did not succeed when it was first tried out with a tax authority other than J. K. Lasser. However, once again Leon Shimkin would not take no for an answer and he asked J. K. Lasser to write the guide. (Years later Yoc Lasser told me how he was directed by Leon Shimkin to keep the guide as simple and readable as possible. "Write short sentences and use one-syllable words whenever possible" was one of Leon's instructions.) This time the guide took off and remained the number-one annual throughout the years.

In the 1930s Dick Simon took a trip to Europe and was impressed by the number of paperback publications that were being distributed on a mass-market basis. He wondered why paperback publishing could not be tried in the United States, and he discussed the idea with Max Schuster and Leon Shimkin when he returned. Albert Leventhal, who was then sales manager of Simon and Schuster, was asked to survey American booksellers about their reaction to paperback publishing, and the almost unanimous consensus was negative: the American public would not throw its money away on cheaply produced books; lending libraries (a big thing in those Depression days) would not buy them; schools would not adopt them, etc. Dick Simon's answer to Albert Leventhal when he heard those reports was simply, "Oh, boy, are they wrong!" (That's a phrase, incidentally, that has taken its place in my memory along with Max Schuster's "That's only a detail!")

At any rate, despite Dick Simon's unshaken belief in paperback publishing, the idea remained on the shelf until Leon Shimkin decided to do something about it. He knew that Dick and Max were too busy with regular trade publishing to become personally involved in the formation of a paperback firm, so he decided to try to find the ideal person who could carry the ball. That person turned out to be Robert F. de Graff, a man who had years of experience in low-priced book publishing. He piloted the Garden City Publishing Company, a leader and pioneer in the clothbound, nonfiction reprint field for twelve years. Then he became president of Blue Ribbon Books, another house that specialized in low-priced clothbound editions.

Together with Dick Simon and Max Schuster, Bob de Graff and Leon Shimkin founded Pocket Books and started the paperback revolution in the United States. From 1939 on when they first started, books became as available as cigarettes or toothpaste. By 1950 Leon Shimkin assumed the presidency of Pocket Books and later merged it with Simon and Schuster, of which he had become sole owner.

Lest this begin to look like a biography of Leon Shimkin, I will close this section with the story of only one more of his achievements. I must include it because it is so relevant to the theme and purpose of this book. It is the story of the beginning of low-priced, mass-market juvenile books in this country.

Some forty-odd years ago Leon Shimkin was looking around for bedtime stories to read to his children. He quickly noted that despite the paperback revolution which now made the classics available to the public at the standard Pocket Books price of twenty-five cents, children's books were relatively expensive. Also, even if you could afford them in those Depression days, there weren't that many outlets throughout the country where they were sold.

Well, put yourself in Leon Shimkin's place. What would you have done, particularly after the Pocket Books experience? You guessed it: look for the ideal person to head a juvenile book firm and persuade Dick Simon and Max Schuster to put their money behind it. You see how simple it is to "revolutionize" the customs of the people of this country in a constructive way? I don't mean that facetiously. The founding of Golden Books (or Little Golden Books as they were first known) was a simple idea resulting from a person's simple need: to read inexpensive, easily available children's stories to his son and daughter.

As I said, put yourself in Leon Shimkin's place—not in the past, but (figuratively speaking) in the present—and you'll be amazed at what wonderful things you will be able to accomplish.

When Leon Shimkin challenged the Internal Revenue Service he was certainly exercising the 13th principle. In getting the ball rolling on the paperback revolution as well as the low-priced children's book field, he was using the 9th principle. When he took Dale Carnegie's course he was obviously using a combination of principles 17 and 18. Above all, by constantly taking the initiative in organizing new ventures he was making the most of principle 19.

Richard L. Simon

If you have read the previous pages in this book, you now know quite a few things about Dick Simon, including the fact that he cofounded Simon and Schuster while still in his twenties. And, to emphasize what I indicated before, the purpose of these profiles is not to sketch the biographical facts per se, but solely to use them as the skeletons upon which to flesh out the principles which I want to put before you.

Therefore, in the case of Dick Simon, further details about his career would not be meaningful. However, there are certain things that he said and did that epitomize the philosophy of this book.

In the first place, he was a man of many and varied interests. He was an excellent pianist, photographer, and bridge player, to name a few, and of course he had a great passion for books. On several occasions I was with him when he would walk into a bookstore and buy a book that he could have got free of charge from the publisher. He preferred to give the author, publisher, and bookseller a break. However, it was the slogan "Give the reader a break" for which everyone remembers him. He tried to carry out those words not only with respect to the editing and manufacturing of books, but with the advertising, promotion, and pricing as well.

With respect to the pricing of books, it is ironic—or at least fascinating—that in 1939 the cheapest as well as the most expensive books in trade publishing were published because of Dick Simon. The cheap ones were the Pocket Books paperbacks of course; the most expense trade book was *A Treasury of Art Masterpieces* edited by Thomas Craven. That book was the first ten-dollar book issued for the regular trade market, and Dick Simon scribbled the words "I hope we don't lose our shirts on this!" when he initialed the publishing proposal for it.* I was struck by the fact that he took what was then a tremendous risk so blithely.

I learned something else from Dick Simon that saddens me when I think of it, but it is too important to omit. As I indicated before, this book is not the place to discuss the machinations and office politics that were part of the history of Simon and Schuster. However, as a result of office politics Dick Simon told me something that taught me a great deal about human relations. It came about like this: I noted that several key executives for whose careers he had done so much, and who once seemed to idolize him, suddenly seemed to want to thwart him in every way. Their attitude was mind-boggling to me and I couldn't help asking Dick Simon (who knew exactly what was going on behind his back) to explain their behavior to me.

*That book also launched the high-priced art-book revolution in this country.

Surprisingly, he did not talk of those backbiting executives as being the ingrates I thought they were, but instead spoke sympathetically of their actions and gave me the following explanation. He said that when he was a young man he idolized his father and thought of him as a "rock of Gibraltar." However, some years later when his father became old and infirm, Dick Simon found himself in the position of being a father to his father, as opposed to the other way around; and he resented it. He resented the discovery that someone who had once been one of his idols—his father—had developed feet of clay. Likewise, Dick Simon went on to say, when those executives at Simon and Schuster found out that he wasn't always right in his business decisions, they resented the loss of someone they had considered a rock of Gibraltar in *their* lives and acted as immaturely as children. We don't like to see any weaknesses in any of our idols. When we do—as we often must—we have a tendency to exaggerate our resentment at having lost a pillar that provided a feeling of security. Perhaps that is why we so often hurt the ones we love.

At the outset I implied the use of the 18th principle by Dick Simon as a man of so many and varied interests. However, this piece shows that he also was a man who studied the motivations of people and therefore was a practitioner of the 7th principle.

I hope you will undertake the exercise I recommended at the outset; see if you can express the key principles that accounted for the various successes. Whenever you have the opportunity to read capsule biographies of prominent people (usually in newspapers and magazines), practice the same exercise and you will be amazed to confirm that people as different as night and day can use the same strategies for success. Finally, write profiles of your own.

10

PUTTING IT ALL TOGETHER: THE MAGIC OF WISHING FOR WHAT YOU WANT

In the Introduction to this book I indicated that the act of wishing is one of the key elements involved in achieving our aims. The first, and most overlooked, is the self-analysis required for us to *know* what to wish for; the second is knowing exactly what to do in order to achieve our aims, and these are the kinds of techniques most widely written about in all the famous inspirational books. When we have done our homework on the first two elements, we are ready for the act of wishing to produce its magical effects.

I have been using the words *magic* and *magical* for this reason: when a magician does a trick without explaining the secret of his performance, the effect seems magical. Once explained, however it all seems so simple. Similarly, the act of wishing, properly performed, produces effects that seem magical, yet it is all so simple when you know how.

When we make a wish we are actually expressing a preference for one thing, or event, as opposed to another; in a sense we are exercising an option when we choose what to wish for. The more preferences or options that we have to choose from, the more likely is it that one of our wishes will come true. For example, a person stranded on a desert island would not be likely to spend much time wishing to become a great violinist. That person would probably have *one* option: a wish to be rescued.

Being limited to only one wish is a pretty dismal prospect, so it is important for us to increase our options through proper exposure. That is why I outlined the principles of attracting good luck, and also suggested ways to try doing different things to broaden your options.

After several chapters relative to the self-analysis and introspection involved in learning what we want and controlling our lives, I turned to the subject of the tools, or principles, that are available to us in getting the things we want out of life. In chapter 6, "Mental Judo," I tried to show that we have not only our own strengths and talents available to us, but also the mental faculties and abilities of those with whom we have any kind of relationship. We don't have to keep reinventing the wheel all the time; we can "borrow" the strengths of others as long as we are willing to be gracious about it and appreciative of their contribution.

I then reached chapter 8 in which I pointed out that setbacks are not only a part of our lives, but in most cases are the very catalysts that account for the good things that happen. For example, Arthur Godfrey is said to have had the greatest impact on the future course of television programming. Do you know that he, while still in his early days on radio, suffered a near-fatal automobile accident that almost ended his career before it got off the ground? What happened was this: during his months of confinement in a hospital bed he decided to listen as much as possible to all the other radio personalities and find out what he could learn from them. The result was that he decided to change his previous conventional, conservative style to one that was mostly ad lib and informal, and that was the style that catapulted him to the top of the television totem pole. If he had surrendered to the setback in his life instead of trying to profit from it, God only knows what he and the rest of us would have missed.

I bring up the Arthur Godfrey story for another reason besides the "setback to success" principle: it reinforces the fact that "it's not *what* you do but the *way* you do it" that often counts, as I wrote at the end of chapter 5. Also, speaking of Arthur Godfrey leads very smoothly to a word about Dr. Leo Buscaglia, a man whose reputation and impact are growing every day.

Recently when he was a guest on the *Phil Donahue* show, I heard Dr. Buscaglia say that he wasn't saying anything that hadn't been said before; he was not trying to come up with totally new truths or unique philosophic doctrines. His exact words, as I recall them, were, "I haven't said anything that wasn't said before."

Nevertheless, whenever you hear Dr. Buscaglia in person, you feel as though you are receiving a new message; you feel as though you have been shown a new road on which to travel in your quest for the blessings that life has to offer. Phil Donahue remarked that no one else could read the lectures of Leo Buscaglia and give the words the same impact as Leo himself can. He has a gift of communication that is so unique it cannot be duplicated. The result is that we *listen* when he talks, we *think* about what he says, and ultimately we *act* upon his urgings.

The same was true of Arthur Godfrey. It wasn't *what* he said so much as the *way* he said it. That is why, according to Andy Rooney who eulogized him at the end of a *60 Minutes* program, there is no use putting Arthur Godfrey's words on paper for someone else to read. They won't mean any more than Leo Buscaglia's lectures delivered by somebody else.

The point is this: each of us is unique and we must learn to treasure that uniqueness. We must not bury it because we are afraid to look different. Our individuality is the only thing we have, and that is what we must preserve if we are to be true to ourselves.

Remember that you don't have to be a weirdo to be unique. You don't have to go out of your way to be original in order to be true to yourself. Leo Buscaglia says things that have been said before. Beethoven wasn't afraid to sound like Mozart; Picasso wasn't afraid to paint like his predecessors. (Too many contemporary artists and musicians fail to communicate because they do artificial things in the effort to be original. As a result they themselves are the only ones who can appreciate their "creations.") You will be unique, original, a oner—call it what you will—if you find out what really pleases *you* and aren't ashamed to admit it. If you are a rational person who lives in the real world, your tastes will be influenced by the significant expressions of your predecessors and contemporaries; they will not appear to have sprung from some bizarre planet in an unheard-of galaxy as seems to have been the case with so many modern works of "art."

What I am saying is, "Be yourself," one of the simplest, yet profoundest, statements I ever heard. And one of the best ways to be yourself is to compare yourself to others, particularly those whose achievements you admire. That is why I devoted the preceding chapter to some of the people I know who started at the bottom and worked their way to the top. By drawing even a relatively superficial outline of their accomplishments or personal characteristics, I am able to trace the application of those principles I have been espousing throughout this book; and I am better able to respond effectively to whatever opportunities may present themselves to me.

Also, I want to reiterate the importance of learning to live in the present, not the past or the future. You must think about the past and the future from time to time, but you must do your *living* in the present. Keep on challenging your past assumptions and creating new hopes for the future, but don't let yourself "escape" from the present by becoming too preoccupied with those surrounding dimensions.

The *magic* of wishing, knowing what you want and getting it, results from a frame of mind, from a certain outlook or way of looking at things. I hope that everything you have been reading in this book has paved the way for that outlook or frame of mind to manifest itself so that all of your heartfelt wishes may come true. I sincerely hope so, and I promise you that that will happen as you begin to apply the principles and follow the advice that I have collected for you in this book. While I may not have said anything you didn't already know, I am sure the manner in which I have arranged the subject matter of this book is unique and calculated to fulfill the promise of its title.

In music the same notes are used over and over again to produce different effects and stimulate different kinds of feelings in the listener. In this book I have said things that have been said over and over again, but I have orchestrated them in such a way as to produce an original effect—one that will guide you toward your goals for the rest of your life.

CHECKLIST OF PRINCIPLES

At the outset I said that even though different groups of words can mean the same thing, they would not necessarily affect people the same way. When I first took up golf I was admonished to keep my left arm straight when hitting the ball. Somehow I found that difficult to do until I came across a book entitled *Swing the Handle and Not the Clubhead* by Eddie Merrins. That title was all I had to think about when I got ready to swing and I automatically kept my left arm straight.

That is why I reiterated many of the following principles throughout the book but in different words and with different examples. For instance, on page 38 I wrote that I set one of Walt Kelly's lyrics to music *before* he had actually agreed to collaborate with me; on page 81 I told of my friend who took orders for greeting cards *before* starting a greeting card company; on page 101 I indicated how Bob Gottlieb acted as though he were a publisher *before* he actually got the job. All three exemplify the same principle in different ways, one of which may drive the point home more meaningfully to you than the others. We each respond to different *code* words and I want to be sure that I have zeroed in on *yours*.

Finally, I thought it might be a good idea to list a few of the most important principles I discussed, so here they are in the form of a convenient reminder.

1. Keep a lookout for all the principles of behavior that can be learned from the least likely sources: cookbooks, nursery rhymes, as well as texts on psychology.

2. Question the details of the minutiae of your life—the kind of toothbrush or shoehorn you use, etc.—as a first step in learning your true desires.

3. Attract good luck by applying the principles of

exposure, recognition, and response to your daily life.

4. Keep a short but frequent diary of your thoughts in order to evaluate the changes that are occurring with respect to your philosophy of life.

5. Learn what is going on in your subconscious by attempting to recall and analyze your dreams.

6. Control your life by doing your best at whatever you are doing or else not doing it at all.

7. Question whether you are seeing people for what they are or if you are granting them the attributes you wish them to possess.

8. Concentrate on the present as opposed to living in a state of reminiscence or anticipation.

9. Use the heads of others as well as your own by applying Mental Judo appropriately.

10. Do not attempt to ingratiate yourself by offering favors; *ask* for them instead.

11. Study the forest before you study the trees.

12. Always precede statements of criticism or advice with statements of sympathy and understanding.

13. Constantly challenge your long-held assumptions in order to think in three dimensions (laterally) instead of just one.

14. Your liabilities are likely to become your greatest assets.

15. Thwart your built-in will to fail by acting as though it were impossible to fail.

16. Question whether you are aiming for what you really want as opposed to what you think you want.

17. Change and rearrange the details of your life in personal as well as business matters, and face the risks involved with confidence.

18. Make it your business to learn new things, meet new people; try doing many different things, and read books on a variety of subjects.

19. Try to assume the responsibilities and obligations of any office you want *before* you are required to do so.

20. Learn as much as you can about the key people in the field of your interest.

Note that I did not list principles for thinking positively and thinking big, although I did mention those in the book. I omitted them from the checklist because if you follow the 11th principle and the 15th, you will automatically be thinking big as well as positively.

I have presented all the information I have gathered through the years on how to know what you want and get it. If you give my suggestions a try, I promise you that you will be amazed at the results. That is my foremost wish and I hope you will do your best to make that wish come true.